T0054363

DASH DIET AIR FRYER COOKBOOK

DASH Diet
AIR FRYER
COOKBOOK

75 Easy Recipes
for a Healthier Lifestyle

CHRISTINA LOMBARDI, MS, RD, FMNS

Photography by Hélène Dujardin

ROCKRIDGE
PRESS

Copyright © 2022 by Rockridge Press, Oakland, California

No part of this publication may be reproduced, stored in a retrieval system, or transmitted in any form or by any means, electronic, mechanical, photocopying, recording, scanning, or otherwise, except as permitted under Sections 107 or 108 of the 1976 United States Copyright Act, without the prior written permission of the Publisher. Requests to the Publisher for permission should be addressed to the Permissions Department, Rockridge Press, 1955 Broadway, Suite 400, Oakland, CA 94612.

Limit of Liability/Disclaimer of Warranty: The Publisher and the author make no representations or warranties with respect to the accuracy or completeness of the contents of this work and specifically disclaim all warranties, including without limitation warranties of fitness for a particular purpose. No warranty may be created or extended by sales or promotional materials. The advice and strategies contained herein may not be suitable for every situation. This work is sold with the understanding that the Publisher is not engaged in rendering medical, legal, or other professional advice or services. If professional assistance is required, the services of a competent professional person should be sought. Neither the Publisher nor the author shall be liable for damages arising herefrom. The fact that an individual, organization, or website is referred to in this work as a citation and/or potential source of further information does not mean that the author or the Publisher endorses the information the individual, organization, or website may provide or recommendations they/it may make. Further, readers should be aware that websites listed in this work may have changed or disappeared between when this work was written and when it is read.

For general information on our other products and services or to obtain technical support, please contact our Customer Care Department within the United States at (866) 744-2665, or outside the United States at (510) 253-0500.

Rockridge Press publishes its books in a variety of electronic and print formats. Some content that appears in print may not be available in electronic books, and vice versa.

TRADEMARKS: Rockridge Press and the Rockridge Press logo are trademarks or registered trademarks of Callisto Media Inc. and/or its affiliates, in the United States and other countries, and may not be used without written permission. All other trademarks are the property of their respective owners. Rockridge Press is not associated with any product or vendor mentioned in this book.

Interior and Cover Designer: Scott Petrower
Art Producer: Megan Baggott
Editor: Anne Goldberg
Production Editor: Matthew Burnett
Production Manager: Holly Haydash

Photography © 2022 Hélène Dujardin. Food styling by Ashley Strickland. Darren Muir, p. viii; Marija Vidal, p. x, 120; Moya McAllister, p. 17.

Cover recipes: Crispy Lemon-Dijon Cod with Greek Yogurt Sauce, page 98; Quinoa-Chicken Meatballs with Garlicky Zucchini Spirals, page 74

Paperback ISBN: 978-1-63807-960-6
eBook ISBN: 978-1-63807-290-4
R0

To my husband and daughter, for all your support and mutual love for food! Thank you for inspiring me to create healthy, delicious meals.

Contents

Introduction

Welcome! I'm Christina, a registered dietitian and functional medicine nutritionist. If you are reading this book, you are most likely interested in the benefits of the DASH diet and/or looking for new healthy recipes that can be cooked in your air fryer. My goal is to make air frying DASH-compliant foods enjoyable and simple.

I understand how confusing and overwhelming it can be when you are first diagnosed with a medical condition. When I worked as a clinical nutritionist for Stony Brook University Hospital's Heart Institute, I provided medical nutrition therapy for individuals with cardiac conditions such as hypertension, educating them on the DASH diet. Many times, I was the first person a patient met with after a new diagnosis to discuss diet and lifestyle changes. Although it's very common for someone to feel overwhelmed and unsure of how to implement changes after a diagnosis, I found that patients felt less daunted and were able to adjust to new dietary and lifestyle habits easily when we introduced small, consistent changes over a period of time.

I currently own a private practice that provides weight-management nutrition therapy, and I help individuals who are coping with various cardiometabolic conditions. My nutrition practice's approach is centered around a Hippocrates quote, "Let food be thy medicine and medicine be thy food." I believe many medical conditions—such as high blood pressure, for example—can be managed through adopting a healthy diet and lifestyle.

I recently started using the air fryer when I was seeking ways to make healthier versions of some traditionally high-fat meals. Through trial and error, I found the air fryer created flavorful meals that are loaded with nutrients and can easily support the DASH diet. What I love about the DASH diet is that it focuses mostly on what you *can* eat, without being too restrictive with what you *can't*.

The DASH diet is widely prescribed by doctors for patients with high blood pressure, for general cardiac health, and even for weight loss. This diet pattern provides healthy, balanced meals, which will promote sustainable long-term lifestyle habits. By incorporating the air fryer, you can still get the crisp flavor of foods you love without all the added fat and calories.

In this book, you will see guidelines and health benefits for the DASH diet, easy and delicious recipes for any air fryer, healthy ingredients that are easy to find in your local grocery store, and recipes that focus on whole foods.

Chapter 1

DASH to Your Air Fryer

This first chapter is here to familiarize you with the DASH diet and how to use your air fryer. Whether you're totally new to the DASH diet and/or air fryer or you're just looking for some new recipes, this chapter will help you feel prepared and ready to dive into your air fryer and DASH diet lifestyle.

DASH Primer

DASH stands for Dietary Approaches to Stop Hypertension. Researchers at the National Heart, Lung, and Blood Institute of the National Institutes of Health (NIH) created the diet to prevent and treat high blood pressure. The eating pattern focuses on foods rich in potassium, calcium, magnesium, and protein while limiting sodium, saturated fats, and added sugars; it helps reduce blood pressure by either removing excess salt or relaxing the blood vessels to allow better blood flow throughout the body. The DASH diet is shown in research to benefit heart health and lower blood pressure by providing a general healthy diet pattern.

Benefits

It is important to mention at this point that the DASH diet is a guideline and pattern rather than a strict diet; approaches can vary. In addition, it is not a restrictive "crash diet." The goal is to provide long-term health benefits through building sustainable dietary changes and habits. Here we'll take a look at some of those benefits.

Lower blood pressure

Substantial research undertaken by the NIH shows a reduction in blood pressure for individuals with higher-than-normal blood pressure readings who adopt the DASH diet. One study, named the DASH-Sodium Trial, measured blood pressure among patients on the DASH diet with differing sodium intake levels. They found that even at higher sodium intake levels, the DASH diet lowered blood pressure.

Improved heart health

The DASH diet focuses on heart-healthy, anti-inflammatory fats such as omega-3 fatty acids, which promote heart health and improve lipid levels. In addition, by consuming more produce, you will be getting more antioxidants, which are also great for heart health.

Diabetes prevention

The DASH diet emphasizes foods with a low glycemic index and limits food and beverages with added sugars; the glycemic index measures how much a food will raise your blood glucose levels after consumption. When you focus on nutrient-dense foods high in fiber and protein, your blood sugar levels will be better regulated and your risk of developing diabetes will decrease.

Weight loss

The DASH diet involves making small, manageable dietary and lifestyle changes that are flexible and backed by research. This sort of health pattern results in long-term diet adherence, which promotes weight loss and weight management. Lean proteins and fiber help you feel full and can reduce caloric intake, resulting in weight loss.

Improved digestion

Fiber consumed through whole grains and produce feeds the good bacteria in your digestive tract, promotes regular bowel movements, and increases gastric motility, which can reduce digestive symptoms such as constipation and heartburn. It's likely that you will experience greater digestive health while following the DASH diet.

Better sleep

There is more and more research supporting a connection between the DASH diet and better sleep. Typically, high fiber intake is associated with better sleep patterns, whereas foods higher on the glycemic index can cause poor sleep. In addition, magnesium-rich foods, which are plentiful in the DASH diet, can help the body relax and promote more restful sleep.

DASH Principles

The DASH diet was originally designed to lower blood pressure, but it has many other health and cardiovascular advantages. It can be a way of eating for everyone in the household, and it can promote weight loss and reduce the risk of heart disease. Here are the principles at the core of the DASH diet:

Choose lean proteins. Pick poultry, fish, and vegetarian protein sources over fattier proteins. Treat your proteins as a small part of your meal and not the focus. Allow nuts, seeds, whole grains, and vegetables to take center stage. Plant-based, protein-rich foods provide fiber and many vitamins and minerals. Try using beans (e.g., lentils and chickpeas) or nuts and seeds (e.g., almonds, chia, and hemp seeds) for protein sources. Using the air fryer, it's easy to quickly cook delicious proteins such as crispy, juicy chicken tenders while slashing the fat and calories.

Eat a variety of whole grains and starchy vegetables. Carbohydrates such as whole-grain pasta, quinoa, brown rice, squashes, and sweet potatoes provide slow-burning energy and are high in fiber. Limit refined grains like white rice and white flour products. The air fryer will save you a great deal of time when cooking starchy vegetables.

Eat less salt. The DASH diet limits sodium to between 1,500 milligrams (mg) and 2,300 mg daily. Just 1 teaspoon of salt has about 2,300 mg of sodium! Instead of turning to your saltshaker, add flavor to your food by swapping in lemon juice; fresh or dried herbs such as bay leaf, dill, rosemary, paprika, sage, and basil; or red pepper flakes, black pepper, or cayenne for spice without the added sodium. If you aren't sure what level of sodium intake is right for you, talk to your doctor.

Eat a rainbow of fruits and vegetables. Fruits and vegetables are a great source of potassium, calcium, magnesium, and fiber, all of which contribute to lower blood pressure. Different colors can indicate different nutrients and health benefits, so enjoy a rainbow of foods and aim for a variety of colorful fruits and vegetables daily. If you do not have access to fresh produce, use frozen options without added salt and sugar.

Choose foods with heart-healthy fats. Limit saturated fats, which raise cholesterol levels. These fats are typically solid at room temperature, such as butter or lard, and are also present in fatty meats, poultry skin, and whole-milk products. Instead, eat foods rich in unsaturated fats and anti-inflammatory omega-3 fatty acids, such as olive oil, avocado oil, walnuts, almonds, chia seeds, and hemp seeds, as well as fatty fish such as salmon.

Limit refined carbohydrates, especially sugar, sweets, and sugar-sweetened beverages. Added sugars do not add nutritive value to your diet and can contribute to weight gain. Limit added sugar intake to about 24 grams per day (6 teaspoons) for women and 36 grams per day (9 teaspoons) for men. Eat fruit for dessert instead of baked goods, and drink water and low-fat or dairy-alternative milks with meals instead of soda.

Building your plate does not have to be complicated. The DASH diet focuses on balanced meals with the proper portions of protein, carbohydrates, and fat, but you do not need a calculator or food scale to figure out your portions. Simply build your meal by following these guidelines: Using a standard dinner-size plate (about 10 inches), fill half your plate with non-starchy vegetables (e.g., leafy greens, broccoli, peppers, or onions); one-quarter of your plate with grains, starchy vegetables, and/or fruits (e.g., brown rice, quinoa, sweet potato, butternut squash, apples, or berries); and one-quarter of your plate with lean proteins or plant-based proteins. Use fresh herbs or salt-free seasonings to bring bold flavors to your meals. Some great options from this book include One-Basket Chicken with Lemon-Garlic Broccoli and Herbed Potatoes (page 71) and Lemon-Basil Sea Bass with Roasted Tomatoes (page 88).

Get the Most Out of Your Air Fryer

The air fryer is a popular kitchen gadget. Many love the appliance because of its ability to create tasty meals with fewer calories, less mess, and faster cooking times, and these same qualities make it ideal for the DASH diet. Check out some of the benefits of using the air fryer.

Healthier: The air fryer can help you create healthier meals because it uses up to 80 percent less fat than conventional frying. The method of air frying foods uses circulating hot air to crisp the foods rather than oil, so you still get the mouthfeel of fried foods but with fewer calories.

Less mess: Love to cook, but don't love the cleanup? Great news: The air fryer provides one-pan cooking with very little mess. Say goodbye to oil splattering on your countertops, never mind having to drain and dispose of messy oil. Look forward to having just one pot to clean.

Crispy and juicy "fried" foods: The heating system in the air fryer circulates hot air to create a crispy outer coating on foods while trapping the juices in the center, resulting in a tender, flavorful meal and healthier chicken tenders, fish sticks, and vegetable chips.

Faster cooking: The way the heat circulates in the air fryer cuts cooking time by up to 25 percent. This means you can spend less time in the kitchen and more time enjoying your healthy food and engaging in other pleasurable activities.

Cook almost anything: If you can cook it in the oven, you can cook it in the air fryer. The air fryer is a wonderfully versatile appliance. It's best known as a deep-frying alternative, but many air fryer models come programmed with other functions, such as roast, dehydrate, and bake.

Safe: A huge benefit is that the air fryer does not use open flames, like a grill. Also the air fryer does not heat up the whole house like when you're using an oven, which we can all appreciate during the warmer summer months.

Air Fryer 101

Interestingly, air fryers do not actually fry food; instead, they cook using convection heat. Convection heat can reduce cooking times by up to 25 percent or more compared to standard oven cooking.

The most common types of air fryers on the market are basket-type air fryers and convection air fryer ovens. Basket-type air fryers are more compact and have a perforated basket that you place into the appliance, whereas oven-style air fryers have a tray and usually some additional features, such as baking and roasting.

Air fryers come in many different sizes. Choosing the correct size for you or your family will ensure that your air fryer is suited to your needs and gets used often. For the solo home chef, look for an air fryer that is around 2 quarts in size, which will be enough to hold a chicken breast and a side of vegetables. For two people, a 3-quart air fryer will provide enough space. If you're cooking for three or more, consider upgrading to a 6- to 10-quart air fryer. The large size can even roast a whole chicken.

The air fryer is a great alternative to deep-frying; however, its versatility allows it to cook all sorts of foods you may not have even considered.

Beans: Beans can get extra crispy in the air fryer in less than 10 minutes.

Burgers: Juicy burgers are made with ease in the air fryer. There is no open flame to deal with and very little mess. In my opinion, air-fried burgers taste even better than those cooked on a grill.

Desserts: Desserts are a breeze to make in the air fryer, and baking time may be reduced by up to 50 percent.

Fish: Air frying fish cuts down on cooking time while delivering a crispy exterior and juicy, tender interior.

Fruit: Does this surprise you? Air frying fruit can provide a caramelized treat without the added sugar.

Lean proteins: Proteins you typically would cook in an oven can be cooked up to 40 percent faster in the air fryer.

Vegetables: Cubed squashes, root vegetables, broccoli, and Brussels sprouts are just some of the vegetables that can be prepared in the air fryer, and you can adjust the cooking time to achieve crisp, savory perfection.

Using Your Air Fryer

Congratulations on your air fryer purchase! First things first: Be sure to read over the owner's manual. Air fryer models will differ, and the manual will give you information specific to your appliance. Go over these notes prior to using your air fryer, and refer back here as you get acquainted with your new appliance.

Clean the appliance before using: Remove all the packaging from the air fryer, including any plastic. Be sure to wash the removable pieces of the appliance, including the basket, with warm soapy water before using it for the first time. Use a soft sponge and nonabrasive cleaners or pads to avoid harming the surfaces.

Test run: I suggest doing a test run before using your appliance to cook. Doing this will help you become familiar with your air fryer and make sure it's working correctly. Check that the basket is empty and that the air fryer is plugged in, then set the temperature to 400°F and the timer for 5 minutes. Once the cycle has run, carefully pull out the hot basket and let it cool for 5 minutes.

Preheating: Check your owner's manual to see if your air fryer needs to be preheated before use.

Preset settings: Some air fryers come with preset settings, such as steak, chicken, and french fries. These can make cooking easier; however, the recipes in this book do not use any preset settings. You will be provided with a temperature and cooking time for every recipe.

Ensure even cooking: When recipes call for sliced foods, such as vegetables, be sure to cut the foods into similar-size pieces so that they cook evenly. When possible, leave space around food in the basket and always evenly spread out the food in a single layer for best results.

Beware of overcooking: Periodically check the food to ensure you are not overcooking anything. It's important to note that there may be some cooking time variations between different air fryer models, but the recipes in this book will notify you when to expect your food to be done.

Best basket practices: Some foods require you to shake the basket during cooking. If applicable, this will be noted in the recipes and usually is noted within the user manual as well for specific foods. Remember, the basket is extremely hot during cooking and after use, so don't forget to use oven mitts or silicone pads when touching the basket. Use tongs or a fork to remove the food from the basket, rather than flipping the basket over.

Air Fryer FAQ

As with any appliance, especially if you haven't used it before, it's common to have some questions. Here are some of the most frequently asked, along with their answers.

1. **Do you need to preheat the air fryer?** Be sure to check your owner's manual to see if preheating your air fryer is required, because different models will vary. However, the recipes will indicate when preheating is needed.

2. **Can you air fry food that is frozen?** The air fryer is great for frozen foods, because it heats the food faster than conventional ovens, although many frozen and processed foods may not be DASH-compliant.

3. **Can you air fry without using any oil at all?** Yes, you can; the circulation of the heat will still brown the food and provide a crispy texture. However, I find it's best to lightly mist some foods or the air fryer basket with oil, as indicated in the recipes, to prevent any sticking, add flavor, and encourage browning.

4. **Is air frying healthier than deep-frying?** The air fryer is a healthier way to cook than deep-frying because of the way the appliance uses convection heat to cook and brown the food. This requires up to 80 percent less oil and results in a lower-calorie dish.

5. **How do you clean the air fryer?** Always clean the appliance after every use. Turn the air fryer off, unplug it, and allow it to cool completely, then wipe the inside with a moist cloth if necessary. Check the manual to see if the basket and removal pieces are dishwasher safe; if not, soak them in warm soapy water and clean with a nonabrasive sponge.

Accessorize Your Air Fryer

There are many accessories that can simplify cooking in your air fryer. Some models may come with accessories included, but in case yours doesn't, here are five of my favorites.

Bakeware: The air fryer can act as a super-hot oven, cutting down on baking time. Baking pans measured to fit your particular size of air fryer can make cooking cakes and breads much easier. Muffin tins specifically made for the air fryer also make whipping up a batch of muffins super easy, like with Vegan Pumpkin Muffins (page 113).

Digital food thermometer: Take the guesswork out of doneness. Food thermometers can be found for a reasonable price and will tell you when your food is done.

Grill pan and skewers: In an air fryer, you can cook anything that you would cook on the grill. A grill pan and skewers can provide a two-level shelf, helpful for cooking larger batches of foods.

Oil mister: Oil misters are great for low-fat cooking; you can add your choice of oil to the mister and lightly coat the cooking basket or food. This way, you get the taste but not the extra calories.

Parchment paper: Parchment liners designed specifically for air fryers make cleanup a breeze—just be sure to look for your specific basket measurements to ensure a good fit. You can also use regular parchment paper cut to a size that will fit in your air fryer. Silicone liners are also an option.

Tongs: Turning the air fryer basket upside down to remove food is not recommended, so tongs are an important accessory to have on hand.

Stock a DASH-Friendly Refrigerator and Pantry

Sticking to the DASH diet begins with having a plan! Start with a kitchen makeover; stock up on DASH diet staples and discard noncompliant foods. Remember, it's easier to cook healthy meals when you have healthy foods available. These lists will also help you make better choices when eating out.

Foods to Reach For

One of the great things about the DASH diet is that you can still eat your favorite foods, just in a healthier way. But choosing the items in this list will benefit your health even more.

Condiments and seasonings: Herbs, spices, citrus, and salsa all provide lots of flavor without the sodium. Check the nutrition label on food containers for sodium levels.

Fruits: Enjoy fresh or frozen fruit with no added sugar or salt, such as berries. If choosing canned fruits, look for fruits canned in their own juice, not syrup.

Heart-healthy fats: Healthy fats that help reduce inflammation include extra-virgin olive oil, avocado oil, unsalted nuts and seeds, and avocados, but these should still be limited to 3 or 4 servings per day.

Lean animal proteins: Choose skinless chicken and turkey, egg whites, extra-lean beef, salmon, and bass.

Low-fat dairy: Select low-fat dairy options, such as nonfat or 1% milk, part-skim cheeses, and plain Greek yogurt. When possible, choose products from grass-fed animals, because they contain higher omega-3 fatty acid levels.

Vegetables: Choose a variety of fresh or frozen vegetables with no added sugar or sauces, such as broccoli, spinach, and zucchini.

Whole grains and legumes: Pick rolled or steel-cut oats, quinoa, brown rice, farro, whole-grain pasta, and bread. Remember to check sodium levels in bread products. Enjoy all beans, such as lentils and black beans (choose low-sodium options, if using canned varieties).

Foods to Moderate

I'm a big believer in the 80/20 rule: Follow the dietary guidelines in this book and the DASH diet 80 percent of the time and enjoy food stress-free for the remaining 20 percent of the time, which could equate to 1 or 2 meals per week. Just remember that the 20 percent should not be a free-for-all and should still stay within reason, such as these foods here.

Caffeine: Although the DASH diet does not prescribe a coffee or caffeine limit, caffeine consumption can temporarily raise blood pressure. Limit caffeine intake to no more than 1 to 3 cups per day, unless otherwise directed by your physician.

Fats: Although heart-healthy fats are allowed and recommended on the DASH diet, it's important not to overdo it, so limit fats to 3 or 4 servings daily.

Low-sugar sweets: Frozen Greek yogurt, sherbet, and homemade desserts low in added sugars can all be part of your diet, but limit them to 3 to 5 servings per week.

Sneaky Sodium

The DASH diet limits sodium intake to between 1,500 mg and 2,400 mg per day. For reference, 1 teaspoon of table salt contains roughly 2,300 mg. In addition to avoiding the saltshaker at your dinner table, when purchasing foods, look at the nutrition label on the package, which will list the amount of sodium per serving. (Remember the amount listed is for one serving, which may be more or less than what you actually consume.) A good rule of thumb when looking at the label is to note the sodium listed in milligrams and calories per serving. The sodium per serving should be about the same as the calories per serving. In this way, you likely will not exceed 2,300 calories or milligrams of sodium per day. If the sodium is much higher than the calories, then consider it a high-sodium meal. For example, a can of green beans may be 20 calories and 300 mg sodium per serving; this would be considered a high-sodium food. Many foods naturally contain sodium; however, these levels are much less than foods with added sodium. Plus, foods with naturally occurring sodium also contain other vitamins and minerals.

Foods to Replace

The great benefit of the DASH diet is that it is not overly restrictive. Here are some foods you should avoid, but don't worry, it is easy to replace them with better choices.

High-sodium foods: Canned foods and condiments such as mustard and ketchup tend to be very high in sodium. Choose low-sodium options or build flavor with spices and herbs instead.

Highly processed foods: Frozen microwavable meals and prepared foods such as pizza, deli meats, instant soups, and potato chips are typically high in sodium and/or sugar. Save leftovers from home-cooked meals for a convenient meal you can reheat. Use the air fryer to make healthy chips.

Store-bought baked goods: These are typically high in salt, sugar, and fat (saturated fats), so swap them out for fruits, unsalted nuts, or air-popped popcorn.

Sugary drinks: Soda and fruit drinks provide little or no nutritional value but lots of sugar. Swap for sparkling water, flavored seltzers, or water with lemon or fruit wedges.

The Long-Term Lifestyle

In addition to dietary changes, making some lifestyle modifications will boost the benefits of the DASH diet. Typically, a combination of diet and exercise will yield the best sustainable results for cardiometabolic health, as well as weight management. Research shows people who make small, consistent lifestyle and dietary changes are more likely to sustain these benefits in the long term.

Food Habits

Remember to begin your health journey with small, easy, and doable changes. Simply start by adding the following habits into your daily routine; over time, they will become second nature.

Focus on protein, carbohydrates, and fats at meals and snacks: Combine these macronutrients and create dishes that will keep you feeling full between meals.

Shop the perimeter of the grocery store: Most processed foods do not have to be refrigerated and are positioned in the middle aisles of the store, whereas perishable foods (which are generally less processed) are placed along the outer perimeter.

Drink enough water: Drink half your body weight in ounces of water daily for baseline hydration. The hypothalamus of the brain controls both hunger and thirst. Sometimes, the body can mix up signals sent by the brain—meaning you think you're hungry when you just need some hydration. If for some reason you have to restrict your fluids, follow your physician's orders.

Be present when you are eating: Eat away from distractions such as electronics, and practice mindful eating techniques. Try chewing your food completely and putting your fork down between bites. Focus on the tastes and textures of the food you're eating, and enjoy any company you're with.

Exercise

Exercise in combination with dietary changes will boost the benefits of any program you follow, especially the DASH diet. The benefits of physical activity are immense and include better strength and endurance, stronger heart and lungs, improved well-being, decreased weight gain, and a decrease in blood pressure and risk of diabetes.

Aim for 150 minutes of moderate-intensity physical activity per week. Physical activity can include walking, running, biking, hiking, dancing, sports, and strength training. Always get the go-ahead from your health-care provider before starting a new exercise program.

How can you determine if your physical activity is moderate intensity?

◆ Use a rate of perceived exertion scale: On a scale of 1 to 10, with 10 being the highest, work at a level between 6 and 8.

◆ Use the talk test: It should be difficult to engage in a conversation during moderate-intensity physical activity.

◆ Monitor heart and breathing rate: You should notice an increase in heart and breathing rate during moderate physical activity.

If you are just beginning an exercise program, aim for 30 minutes of physical activity on most days. Break down the 30 minutes per day into three 10-minute sessions. Gradually increase the duration and number of times you exercise every week.

Sleep

Proper sleep is very important for general health and wellness. However, most individuals are not getting enough shut-eye each night. Fortunately, some research indicates that individuals who follow the DASH diet tend to get better sleep. Aim for 7 to 9 hours of good quality sleep each night. This includes feeling rested when you awaken and not waking up during the night.

Here are tips for the best sleep hygiene:

◆ Set up regular sleep and wake patterns to help synchronize your circadian rhythm. Set an alarm as a reminder to start getting ready for bed and another alarm for when to wake.

◆ Power down electronics and television 1 hour before bedtime, because the light from electronics can disrupt sleep patterns. Try relaxing with a book, a warm bath, meditation, journaling, or herbal tea.

◆ Dim all the lights in the house 30 minutes before bed.

◆ Aim for comfort in your bedroom. Make your bedroom electronic-free. Keep your room dark and cool.

About the Recipes

The 75 recipes in this book were chosen to provide you with DASH-compliant, nutrient-dense, tasty, and fun dishes that can all be prepared in the air fryer. These meals can be prepared for one person but are also great to share with family and friends. The chapters are arranged by courses, starting with Breakfast and Brunch and ending with Desserts. Please also take note of the charts in the back of the book. These charts have handy guidelines for temperature and cooking times for some commonly prepared foods, and the measurement conversion charts will help you convert standard measurements as needed. I tested the recipes in this book using a basket-style 6.8-quart air fryer.

All recipes give you the prep and cook times, so you can determine which meals might be best for your busy schedule. It's important to know that cook times may differ across different models of air fryers; if the food is not finished at the end of the recipe's recommended cook time, just add a few more minutes, until it reaches your desired doneness. If your recipe time differs, be sure to jot down the actual time for your future reference.

All recipes will also indicate the air fryer cooking temperature, as well as how much the recipe makes. Most recipes make enough to serve four people; if you're cooking for one, simply cut the recipe in half and you will have delicious leftovers for another day.

Let's check out some of the recipe labels you will see in this book.

30-Minute: Takes no longer than 30 minutes from prep to finish

Dairy-Free: Does not contain any dairy products and may use dairy alternatives

Gluten-Free: Does not contain gluten; appropriate for anyone following a gluten-free diet

Vegan: Does not contain any animal products or by-products

Vegetarian: Does not contain animal products, except dairy and eggs

At the end of some recipes, you'll see tips on how to achieve the best outcome in the air fryer, recipe variations with different flavors or different proteins and vegetables, and some ideas for substitutions to make a dish gluten- or dairy-free.

I'm excited for you to try out these recipes and learn that following the DASH diet can be fun and tasty, as well as healthy. Let's cook!

Breakfasts and Brunches

Best-Ever Egg Muffins

Makes 8 muffins / **Prep time:** 10 minutes / **Cook time:** 20 minutes / **Temperature:** 400°F, then 320°F

30-MINUTE, GLUTEN-FREE, VEGETARIAN

Egg muffins are easy grab-and-go meals, making them great to prepare ahead of time for busy weekdays. Just refrigerate them in an airtight container for up to 4 days or freeze for 1 month. I often make a batch on Sunday and eat them during the first part of the week. The combination of cheddar cheese and butternut squash gives these muffins a tangy and sweet flavor and provides a tasty meal that will keep you feeling satisfied all morning.

2 cups peeled, cubed butternut squash

2 large eggs

10 egg whites

½ cup shredded low-sodium cheddar cheese

2 cups chopped broccoli florets

2 teaspoons dried oregano

¼ teaspoon freshly ground black pepper

¼ teaspoon sea salt

1. Preheat the air fryer to 400°F.

2. Arrange the butternut squash in a single layer in the air fryer basket and cook for 10 minutes.

3. Meanwhile, in a large bowl, whisk together the eggs and egg whites. Add the cheddar cheese, broccoli, oregano, black pepper, and salt to the eggs and stir to combine.

4. Carefully transfer the butternut squash to the egg mixture.

5. Arrange 8 muffin cup liners in a single layer in the basket. (If your air fryer came with silicone muffin cups, you can use those.) Divide the egg mixture between the liners, making sure not to overfill them.

6. Reduce the air fryer temperature to 320°F and cook for 10 minutes. The muffins are done when a knife inserted into the center comes out clean.

AIR-FRYER TIP: I like to use thawed frozen butternut squash cubes or precut fresh squash for this recipe to keep the prep time minimal.

Per serving (2 muffins): Calories: 207; Total fat: 8g; Saturated fat: 4g; Cholesterol: 107g; Sodium: 350mg; Carbohydrates: 17g; Fiber: 5g; Protein: 19g

Chewy Breakfast Cookies

Makes 12 cookies / **Prep time:** 5 minutes / **Cook time:** 10 minutes / **Temperature:** 320°F

30-MINUTE, GLUTEN-FREE, VEGAN

There is something about cookies for breakfast that just makes me happy. This low-sugar version is a great stand-alone meal, or it can be combined with Greek yogurt for something a little more substantial. Chia seeds contain high levels of omega-3 fatty acids, a heart-healthy and anti-inflammatory fat. They are also rich in calcium. The air fryer gives these cookies an extra crispy outside and chewy inside in only 10 minutes.

1 cup gluten-free old-fashioned rolled oats

2 medium ripe bananas, mashed

1 tablespoon unsalted almond butter

2 tablespoons chia seeds

½ teaspoon baking powder

¾ teaspoon pure vanilla extract

¼ teaspoon sea salt

¼ cup dark chocolate chips

1. Preheat the air fryer to 320°F.

2. In a large bowl, stir together the oats, bananas, almond butter, chia seeds, baking powder, vanilla, and salt. Gently fold in the chocolate chips.

3. Working in batches if necessary, drop dough in rounded tablespoonfuls in a single layer directly into the air fryer basket, 1 inch apart. Cook for 10 minutes, or until golden brown. Allow to cool before serving.

VARIATION TIP: Don't have chia seeds? Substitute hemp seeds in this recipe to still get the heart health benefits.

Per serving (3 cookies): Calories: 260; Total fat: 10g; Saturated fat: 3g; Cholesterol: 1g; Sodium: 210mg; Carbohydrates: 38g; Fiber: 7g; Protein: 6g

Classic Turkey Breakfast Hash

Serves 4 / **Prep time:** 10 minutes / **Cook time:** 25 minutes / **Temperature:** 400°F

DAIRY-FREE, GLUTEN-FREE

If you're looking for a savory egg-free breakfast, this dish is a great choice. Breakfast hash is a nutritious one-basket meal that cooks quickly in the air fryer. The combination of turkey, vegetables, and turnips make this meal super satisfying and hearty to keep you going all morning. The spice combination gives the hash great flavor, so you won't miss the ketchup.

1 tablespoon dried basil

1 teaspoon dried oregano

1 teaspoon chili powder

½ teaspoon sweet paprika

½ teaspoon granulated garlic

¼ teaspoon red pepper flakes

¼ teaspoon sea salt

1 pound turnips, washed and cut into ½-inch cubes

Avocado oil cooking spray

12 ounces ground turkey, 99% lean

2 large red bell peppers, seeded and diced

¾ cup finely diced red onion

4 cups fresh spinach

1. Preheat the air fryer to 400°F.

2. In a small bowl, stir together the basil, oregano, chili powder, paprika, garlic, red pepper flakes, and salt.

3. Working in batches if necessary, in a single layer, place the turnips in the air fryer basket, mist with avocado oil, and season with half the spice mixture. Cook for 15 minutes.

4. When the cooking time is done, carefully remove the basket, stir the turnips, then add the ground turkey, bell peppers, and onion and lightly spray with avocado oil. Sprinkle the remaining spice mixture on top.

5. Continue to cook at 400°F for another 5 minutes. Add the spinach, stir or shake the hash mixture, and continue to cook until the turkey is no longer pink, another 5 minutes.

VARIATION TIP: Potatoes can be substituted for the turnips; try different-colored potatoes, such as purple or red skinned, for more nutritional benefits and use the same cook time and temperature.

Per serving: Calories: 212; Total fat: 4g; Saturated fat: 1g; Cholesterol: 60g; Sodium: 322mg; Carbohydrates: 16g; Fiber: 5g; Protein: 30g

Zucchini Quiche with Sweet Potato "Crust"

Serves 4 / **Prep time:** 10 minutes / **Cook time:** 25 minutes / **Temperature:** 400°F, then 350°F

DAIRY-FREE, GLUTEN-FREE, VEGETARIAN

Sweet potato as a crust! This is a game changer. The sweetness of the sweet potato and the crispiness from the air fryer makes for a mouthwatering breakfast you will turn to time and time again. Typically, quiches take over 50 minutes to cook in the oven, but the air fryer cooks it in half the time.

2 medium sweet potatoes, cut into ½-inch-thick slices

Avocado oil cooking spray

10 egg whites

¼ cup unsweetened almond milk

2 medium zucchini, chopped

2 cups cherry tomatoes, quartered

3 cups fresh spinach

1 shallot, finely diced

1 garlic clove, minced

½ teaspoon red pepper flakes

½ teaspoon dried oregano

¼ teaspoon sea salt

1 Roma tomato, sliced

1. Preheat the air fryer to 400°F.

2. Working in batches if necessary, arrange the sweet potato slices in an air fryer baking dish, overlapping them slightly to form a single crust-like layer. Spray with avocado oil. Place the baking dish in the air fryer basket and cook for 10 minutes.

3. Meanwhile, in a large bowl, whisk together the egg whites and almond milk. Add the zucchini, cherry tomatoes, spinach, shallot, garlic, red pepper flakes, oregano, and salt and stir to combine.

4. Once the crust is done, carefully pour the egg mixture into the crust. Top the quiche with the tomato slices.

5. Place the baking dish back in the basket, decrease the temperature to 350°F, and cook for 10 to 15 minutes. The quiche is done when a knife inserted near the center comes out clean. Let it rest for 10 minutes before serving.

Per serving: Calories: 145; Total fat: 1g; Saturated fat: 0g; Cholesterol: 0g; Sodium: 362mg; Carbohydrates: 22g; Fiber: 5g; Protein: 13g

Apple-Turkey Sausage Patties

Makes 12 patties / **Prep time:** 10 minutes / **Cook time:** 10 minutes / **Temperature:** 400°F

30-MINUTE, DAIRY-FREE, GLUTEN-FREE

Many store-bought sausages have preservatives and are high in sodium. The DASH diet recommends avoiding these processed foods, and the air fryer makes it very simple to make a healthier version at home. This sausage pairs great with Sweet Potato Toast with Cinnamon Almond Butter (page 26) or Breakfast Pizza with Cauliflower Crust (page 27) for a complete meal.

12 ounces ground turkey, 93% lean

2 cups frozen baby kale, thawed

2 Gala apples, cored and finely minced

1 tablespoon dried sage

1 tablespoon fennel seed

1 tablespoon dried basil

1 teaspoon garlic powder

1 teaspoon freshly ground black pepper

¼ teaspoon sea salt

1. Preheat the air fryer to 400°F.

2. In a medium bowl, stir together the ground turkey, baby kale, apples, sage, fennel seed, basil, garlic powder, black pepper, and salt. Using damp hands, form the turkey mixture into 9 to 12 equal-size patties.

3. Working in batches if necessary, place the patties in a single layer in the air fryer basket and cook for 10 minutes, flipping halfway through, or until the turkey is no longer pink and has an internal temperature of 165°F.

VARIATION TIP: Ground chicken can work in this recipe as well; just make sure to use chicken breast, which is leaner and lower in fat than dark meat.

Per serving (3 patties): Calories: 245; Total fat: 10g; Saturated fat: 3g; Cholesterol: 86g; Sodium: 232mg; Carbohydrates: 14g; Fiber: 4g; Protein: 24g

Berry Baked Oatmeal with Warm Yogurt Sauce

Serves 4 / **Prep time:** 10 minutes / **Cook time:** 15 minutes / **Temperature:** 320°F

30-MINUTE, DAIRY-FREE, GLUTEN-FREE, VEGETARIAN

If you're not a fan of the consistency of hot cereals but still want the heart-healthy benefits and fiber of oats, this baked oatmeal is a great option. The air fryer crisps the top of the oatmeal, providing a crunchy texture and toasty taste, with a soft middle. If you're avoiding gluten, purchase oats that are certified gluten-free, as there can sometimes be cross contamination during production and packaging.

For the oatmeal

2 cups gluten-free old-fashioned rolled oats

3 cups frozen blueberries, divided

1 large ripe banana, mashed

1 tablespoon grated lemon zest

1 large egg white

½ cup unsweetened almond milk

½ teaspoon pure vanilla extract

¼ teaspoon sea salt

¼ teaspoon baking soda

For the sauce

½ cup fresh mixed berries

1 tablespoon water

½ cup plant-based Greek yogurt

VARIATION TIP: This recipe works well with any berry, frozen or fresh.

To make the oatmeal

1. In a medium bowl, stir together the oats, 2 cups of blueberries, the banana, lemon zest, egg white, almond milk, vanilla, salt, and baking soda.

2. Divide the mixture between four ramekins and top with the remaining 1 cup of blueberries. Set the air fryer temperature to 320°F. Cooking in batches if necessary, set the ramekins in the air fryer and cook for 12 minutes.

To make the sauce

3. While the oatmeal is baking, in a medium saucepan over medium heat, combine the mixed berries and water and cook, stirring occasionally, for 4 minutes, or until the berries start to burst and release their juices.

4. Remove from the heat. Pour the yogurt over the berries and gently stir.

5. Serve the ramekins of warm oatmeal topped with dollops of yogurt sauce.

Per serving: Calories: 296; Total fat: 4g; Saturated fat: 1g; Cholesterol: 0g; Sodium: 275mg; Carbohydrates: 61g; Fiber: 9g; Protein: 8g

Sweet Potato Toast with Cinnamon Almond Butter

Serves 4 / **Prep time:** 10 minutes / **Cook time:** 20 minutes / **Temperature:** 375°F

30-MINUTE, GLUTEN-FREE, VEGAN

The air fryer was made for sweet potato "toast," a low-glycemic alternative to toasted bread. The appliance cooks the sweet potato much faster than a conventional oven or toaster oven, and it guarantees a crispy exterior that rivals the crackly surface of traditional toast. It's a great way to switch up your breakfast routine, and it's versatile enough that you can try many different toppings.

2 medium sweet potatoes, cut lengthwise into ¼-inch-thick slices

Extra-virgin olive oil cooking spray

¼ teaspoon sea salt

6 tablespoons unsalted almond butter

1 to 2 tablespoons ground cinnamon

1. Preheat the air fryer to 375°F.
2. Working in batches if necessary, place the sweet potato slices in the air fryer basket in a single layer, mist with olive oil, and sprinkle with the salt.
3. Cook for 20 minutes, flipping the sweet potatoes halfway through.
4. Carefully remove the sweet potatoes, then layer them with the almond butter and sprinkle with cinnamon to taste.

AIR-FRYER TIP: The trick to perfectly crispy sweet potato toast is the size of the sweet potato slice: Too thick and it will not cook through, but too thin and it will fall apart. Start checking your toast at 15 minutes; it may already be done, depending on how crispy you like it.

VARIATION TIP: You can try many different toppings instead of the almond butter. Add Greek yogurt to the almond butter layer for extra protein, or top the sweet potato toast with an egg. Another option is layering avocado on top for healthy fat or layering Greek yogurt and blueberries.

Per serving: Calories: 201; Total fat: 13g; Saturated fat: 1g; Cholesterol: 0g; Sodium: 184mg; Carbohydrates: 18g; Fiber: 5g; Protein: 6g

Breakfast Pizza with Cauliflower Crust

Serves 4 / **Prep time:** 15 minutes / **Cook time:** 35 minutes / **Temperature:** 375°F

DAIRY-FREE, GLUTEN-FREE

Pizza for breakfast? Yes, please. This breakfast pizza is easy to make and packs in 1 full cup of veggies per serving. Chickpea flour adds extra fiber and protein and is a great way to sneak beans into this nutrient-dense meal.

4 cups riced cauliflower (thawed, if frozen)

1 cup chickpea flour

2 large egg whites

1 teaspoon extra-virgin olive oil

1 tablespoon dried oregano

2 teaspoons fresh basil

1 teaspoon dried onion granules

1 teaspoon granulated garlic

1 teaspoon ground fennel seed

1 teaspoon dried thyme

1 teaspoon red pepper flakes

2 large eggs

4 Apple-Turkey Sausage Patties (page 24)

1. Place the cauliflower rice in a single layer in the air fryer basket. Set the temperature to 375°F and cook for 5 minutes.

2. Once done, remove the cauliflower rice from the air fryer and allow to cool to room temperature. Transfer to a paper towel and squeeze out any extra moisture.

3. Transfer the cauliflower to a large bowl and stir in the chickpea flour, egg whites, olive oil, oregano, basil, dried onion, garlic, fennel seed, thyme, and red pepper flakes to form a dough. The dough will be soft.

4. Lay a piece of parchment paper on the countertop. Place the dough on top and cover it with a second piece of parchment paper. Flatten the dough into two discs, about ½ inch thick. (You can also omit the top layer of parchment paper and use damp hands to avoid sticking.)

5. Working in batches, place one cauliflower crust directly into the air fryer basket and cook for 10 minutes, or until golden brown.

6. When the timer goes off, top the crust with 1 cracked egg and 2 sausage patties. Cook for an additional 5 minutes, or until the white of the egg is thick and set and the yolk is slightly runny. Repeat with the second crust.

VARIATION TIP: This spice combination is my take on pizza seasoning; however, you can substitute a pre-made blend instead. Just be sure to check that it doesn't have added salt. I love Frontier Co-Op salt-free pizza seasoning and use it in many different dishes.

Per serving: Calories: 422; Total fat: 16g; Saturated fat: 4g; Cholesterol: 182g; Sodium: 326mg; Carbohydrates: 32g; Fiber: 9g; Protein: 38g

Green Veggie Breakfast Hash
with Tangy Avocado Sauce

Serves 4 / **Prep time:** 15 minutes / **Cook time:** 15 minutes / **Temperature:** 375°F

30-MINUTE, GLUTEN-FREE, VEGAN

The stars of this meal are the green apples and Delicata squash, which give this dish a sweet flavor. I created the tangy avocado sauce to complement the hash and it sure does deliver! This meal can be served alone or tossed with a protein such as leftover turkey or beans. Double the recipe and share with company or make ahead for the week.

For the hash

1 medium Delicata squash, peeled, seeded, and cut into 1-inch cubes

½ cup chopped red onion

4 cups snap peas

2 small green apples, chopped

1 medium red bell pepper, seeded and chopped

1 teaspoon extra-virgin olive oil

1 tablespoon paprika

1 tablespoon rosemary

¼ teaspoon sea salt

For the sauce

½ cup plant-based Greek yogurt

1 medium Hass avocado

1 teaspoon paprika

1 tablespoon freshly squeezed lemon juice

To make the hash

1. In a large bowl, stir together the squash, onion, snap peas, apples, bell pepper, olive oil, paprika, rosemary, and salt and stir.

2. Place the vegetable mixture in the air fryer basket in a single layer. Set the temperature to 375°F and cook for 10 minutes. Shake or stir the vegetable hash and continue to cook for 5 minutes, until the vegetables are tender.

To make the sauce

3. While the hash is cooking, in a medium bowl, stir together the yogurt, avocado, paprika, and lemon juice. Slightly mash the avocado to soften it, then whisk until everything is smooth and creamy.

4. Top the vegetable hash with the green sauce and enjoy.

Per serving: Calories: 236; Total fat: 9g; Saturated fat: 1g; Cholesterol: 0g; Sodium: 155mg; Carbohydrates: 37g; Fiber: 10g; Protein: 7g

French Toast Sticks with Yogurt-Berry Dipping Sauce

Serves 4 / **Prep time:** 10 minutes / **Cook time:** 10 minutes / **Temperature:** 350°F

30-MINUTE, VEGETARIAN

This healthy twist on French toast uses coconut sugar instead of regular sugar, which has a lower glycemic index, the measure of how much of a food makes your blood sugar rise. The Greek yogurt–berry dipping sauce is a low-sugar alternative to maple syrup and provides some additional protein in this meal.

For the French toast sticks

1 large egg

1 cup unsweetened almond milk

3 tablespoons ground cinnamon

1 tablespoon coconut sugar

4 slices whole-grain bread, each cut into 4 "sticks"

For the sauce

1 cup blueberries

1 tablespoon water

2 cups low-fat Greek yogurt

AIR-FRYER TIP: I used small slices of bread, about ½ inch thick. If your bread is 1 or more inches thick, you'll want to increase the egg mixture by 50 percent.

To make the French toast sticks

1. Preheat the air fryer to 350°F.

2. In a medium bowl, whisk together the egg, almond milk, cinnamon, and coconut sugar.

3. Dip each piece of bread into the egg mixture, dredging it on all sides and making sure it is fully soaked.

4. Cooking in batches if necessary, place the pieces of bread in the air fryer basket in a single layer and cook for 4 minutes. Flip the sticks over and cook for another 3 minutes, or until golden brown.

To make the sauce

5. Meanwhile, in a small saucepan over medium-high heat, combine the blueberries and water and cook, stirring occasionally, for 4 minutes, or until the berries start to burst and release their juices. While still warm, pour the blueberries over the Greek yogurt and gently stir to combine.

6. To serve, dip the French toast sticks in the yogurt-berry sauce while warm.

Per serving: Calories: 278; Total fat: 6g; Saturated fat: 2g; Cholesterol: 57g; Sodium: 264mg; Carbohydrates: 37g; Fiber: 7g; Protein: 21g

Chapter 3

Snacks and Sides

Crispy Avocado Fries with Cilantro Pesto

Serves 4 / **Prep time:** 15 minutes / **Cook time:** 5 minutes / **Temperature:** 370°F

30-MINUTE, VEGAN

Avocados are a nutritional powerhouse, high in heart-healthy monounsaturated fats and fiber. Avocados are classified as a fruit, not a vegetable, and contain no cholesterol. You will find the air fryer gives the avocados in this recipe a nice crispy outer coating, while they stay creamy and soft on the inside. Cilantro is the star of this pesto recipe, providing a fresh, citrusy taste. Leftovers can be used as a marinade for grilled chicken or shrimp, or stirred into a vinaigrette to freshen up salad dressing. Try this dish as a snack or as a side to your main meal.

For the pesto

½ bunch fresh cilantro, stemmed

2 tablespoons extra-virgin olive oil

3 tablespoons pine nuts, lightly toasted and cooled

2 tablespoons freshly squeezed lime juice

½ teaspoon ground cumin

¼ teaspoon sea salt

Freshly ground black pepper

To make the pesto

1. In a high-speed blender or food processor, combine the cilantro, olive oil, pine nuts, lime juice, cumin, and salt and blend on high speed until well mixed. If the mixture appears dry, add water 1 teaspoon at a time until you achieve a smooth, pourable consistency. Season with pepper to taste.

For the avocado fries

¾ cup unsweetened almond milk

1 teaspoon granulated garlic

1 tablespoon whole wheat flour

1 cup whole wheat panko bread crumbs

1 teaspoon paprika

1 teaspoon dried oregano

2 Hass avocados, cut into ⅛-inch wedges

Extra-virgin olive oil cooking spray

To make the avocado fries

2. Preheat the air fryer to 370°F.

3. In a small bowl, whisk together the almond milk, granulated garlic, and whole wheat flour.

4. In another small bowl, stir together the panko bread crumbs, paprika, and oregano.

5. One at a time, dunk each avocado wedge into the almond milk mixture and then coat in the panko bread crumb mixture. Repeat until all wedges have been coated.

6. Working in batches if necessary, arrange the avocado wedges in a single layer in the air fryer basket, making sure not crowd the slices. Mist with olive oil and cook for 3 minutes per side. The fries are done when golden brown and crispy. Serve the fries with the pesto on the side.

AIR-FRYER TIP: This is best made with a ripe but still firm avocado. If the avocado is too soft, it may fall apart in the air fryer.

VARIATION TIP: To make this gluten-free, look for gluten-free panko bread crumbs and use rice flour in place of the whole wheat flour.

Per serving: Calories: 301; Total fat: 22g; Saturated fat: 3g; Cholesterol: 0g; Sodium: 215mg; Carbohydrates: 24g; Fiber: 8g; Protein: 6g

Crispy Rosemary Parsnip Fries

Serves 4 / **Prep time:** 5 minutes / **Cook time:** 10 minutes / **Temperature:** 350°F

30-MINUTE, GLUTEN-FREE, VEGAN

Parsnips are a cream-colored root vegetable related to the carrot. They are a great source of fiber (about 6.5 g per cup). They naturally have a sweet flavor and are an excellent substitute for french fries. The air fryer provides excellent results, giving them the perfect crispy texture in less than 10 minutes.

7 medium parsnips, washed and peeled (about 7 inches long, about 1½ pounds)

2 tablespoons extra-virgin olive oil

3 tablespoons dried rosemary

1 tablespoon granulated garlic

¼ teaspoon sea salt

1. Preheat the air fryer to 350°F.

2. Cut the parsnips lengthwise into ½-inch-thick strips. If you have a mandoline slicer with a fry attachment, set the thickness to ¼ inch and slice.

3. In a large bowl, stir together the parsnips, olive oil, rosemary, and garlic.

4. Working in batches if necessary, transfer the parsnips to the air fryer basket and spread into a single layer. Season with the salt and cook for 9 minutes, giving them a shake or a quick stir halfway through the cooking time.

AIR-FRYER TIP: To ensure a crispy texture, do not crowd the parsnips in the basket.

VARIATION TIP: Spice up this recipe by swapping out the parsnips for carrots and adding spices such as cayenne pepper, garlic, black pepper, and parsley. Cook for the same time and at the same temperature.

Per serving: Calories: 203; Total fat: 8g; Saturated fat: 1g; Cholesterol: 0g; Sodium: 166mg; Carbohydrates: 34g; Fiber: 10g; Protein: 3g

Roasted Balsamic-Parmesan Brussels Sprouts

Serves 4 / **Prep time:** 5 minutes / **Cook time:** 20 minutes / **Temperature:** 350°F

30-MINUTE, GLUTEN-FREE

Brussels sprouts are one of my favorite side dishes. I love them extra crispy, and the air fryer is the perfect cooking method to achieve this texture. Brussels sprouts are part of the cruciferous family (like broccoli and kale) and have strong cancer-fighting properties. They are also high in fiber, which provides bulk to your meal without the extra calories.

1½ pounds Brussels sprouts, trimmed and halved

2 tablespoons extra-virgin olive oil

2 garlic cloves, crushed and chopped

3 tablespoons balsamic vinegar

2 tablespoons grated Parmesan cheese

1. Preheat the air fryer to 350°F.

2. In a medium bowl, stir together the Brussels sprouts, olive oil, and garlic.

3. Working in batches if necessary, layer the Brussels sprouts in a single layer in the air fryer basket and cook for 20 minutes, giving them an occasional stir or shake, until crispy and slightly charred on the outside.

4. Once the timer goes off, drizzle the balsamic vinegar over the Brussels sprouts and cook for another 2 minutes.

5. When done, carefully remove the Brussels sprouts from the basket and sprinkle the Parmesan cheese on top.

AIR-FRYER TIP: Shaking the basket several times throughout cooking will allow the Brussels sprouts to crisp evenly with a tender inside. If you like your Brussels sprouts less crispy, start checking for doneness after 15 minutes.

Per serving: Calories: 159; Total fat: 8g; Saturated fat: 2g; Cholesterol: 3g; Sodium: 102mg; Carbohydrates: 18g; Fiber: 7g; Protein: 7g

Parmesan Broccoli with Walnuts and Basil

Serves 4 / **Prep time:** 5 minutes / **Cook time:** 10 minutes / **Temperature:** 320°F

30-MINUTE, GLUTEN-FREE

Most people love broccoli with cheese on top, so I created this recipe for the cheese lovers with the DASH diet in mind. The lemon, basil, and toasted walnuts provide extra flavor, so not as much cheese is required. The air fryer makes it easy to vary the broccoli's flavor profile based on the cooking time; if you like yours more charred or "burnt" flavored, cook it for a couple minutes extra.

4 cups broccoli florets

3 tablespoons freshly squeezed lemon juice

2 tablespoons extra-virgin olive oil

½ cup walnut halves, chopped

2 garlic cloves, crushed

½ cup minced fresh basil

3 tablespoons grated Parmesan cheese

1. Preheat the air fryer to 320°F.

2. In a medium bowl, stir together the broccoli florets, lemon juice, olive oil, walnuts, and garlic.

3. Working in batches if necessary, arrange the broccoli in a single layer in the air fryer basket and cook for 8 minutes, occasionally stirring or shaking.

4. Once the timer goes off, transfer the broccoli to a large bowl. Top with the basil and Parmesan cheese.

AIR-FRYER TIP: The cook time will result in slightly charred broccoli. If you like more of a burnt texture, continue to cook, checking every 2 minutes, until it is cooked to your liking.

Per serving: Calories: 198; Total fat: 17g; Saturated fat: 3g; Cholesterol: 4g; Sodium: 115mg; Carbohydrates: 10g; Fiber: 3g; Protein: 6g

Roasted Root Veggies with Fresh Oregano

Serves 4 / **Prep time:** 10 minutes / **Cook time:** 20 minutes / **Temperature:** 400°F

30-MINUTE, GLUTEN-FREE, VEGAN

Use this recipe as a side dish or throw leftovers into salads and grain bowls. Although celery is not a root vegetable, it's a great addition here, and roasting it intensifies its flavor and makes it slightly sweet. A bonus to using the air fryer is that it will cut the cooking time by almost half when compared to roasting the veggies in the oven.

1 pound sweet potatoes, cubed

1 medium turnip, peeled and cubed

1 medium beet, peeled and cubed

1 medium red onion, diced

7 celery stalks, chopped

3 tablespoons avocado oil

4 tablespoons stemmed fresh oregano

2 tablespoons ground cinnamon

1. Preheat the air fryer to 400°F.

2. In a large bowl, stir together the sweet potatoes, turnip, beet, onion, celery, avocado oil, oregano, and cinnamon.

3. Working in batches if necessary, arrange the vegetables in a single layer in the air fryer basket and cook for 20 minutes. Shake or stir the vegetables halfway through the cooking time.

VARIATION TIP: Any root vegetables would work great in this recipe. If you have a local farm stand or market, use what is in season in your area and follow the instructions as written.

Per serving: Calories: 242; Total fat: 11g; Saturated fat: 1g; Cholesterol: 0g; Sodium: 190mg; Carbohydrates: 36g; Fiber: 9g; Protein: 4g

Zucchini Chips

Serves 4 / **Prep time:** 10 minutes / **Cook time:** 10 minutes / **Temperature:** 400°F

30-MINUTE, GLUTEN-FREE, VEGAN

These Zucchini Chips are a low-calorie and low-carb snack alternative for potato chips, which have higher fat and salt content. Zucchini are actually green-fleshed fruit and not a vegetable due to their flowers, which are also edible. They are also referred to as summer squash, because they are grown and harvested in the summer in cooler locations. This recipe also uses nutritional yeast, a plant-based food that provides a cheesy flavor to dishes.

3 tablespoons dried basil

½ cup nutritional yeast

¼ teaspoon sea salt

5 large zucchini, cut into ⅛-inch-thick rounds

Avocado oil cooking spray

1. Preheat the air fryer to 400°F.

2. In a small bowl, combine the basil, nutritional yeast, and salt. Set aside.

3. Lay the zucchini slices on a dishcloth or paper towel, cover with another paper towel, and lightly press to remove any excess moisture.

4. Working in batches, arrange the zucchini slices in a single layer in the air fryer basket. Mist with the avocado oil and season with half of the nutritional yeast mixture. Set the temperature to 400°F and cook for 5 minutes.

5. When the timer goes off, flip each zucchini chip, mist with more oil, and season with the remaining nutritional yeast mix. Cook for another 3 minutes.

6. Remove the chips from the basket and allow to cool before eating.

AIR-FRYER TIP: It's best to cut the zucchini into equally thick slices so they cook evenly and prevent burning. A mandoline would work great here.

VARIATION TIP: You can substitute yellow summer squash in this recipe to achieve a slightly sweeter taste.

Per serving: Calories: 192; Total fat: 3g; Saturated fat: 0g; Cholesterol: 0g; Sodium: 191mg; Carbohydrates: 25g; Fiber: 13g; Protein: 22g

Roasted Delicata Squash with Balsamic Drizzle

Serves 4 / **Prep time:** 5 minutes / **Cook time:** 15 minutes / **Temperature:** 400°F

30-MINUTE, GLUTEN-FREE

I first tried Delicata squash just a couple years ago, but it quickly became one of my favorite winter squashes. It has a creamy texture and is sweeter than most other squashes. The skin is thin and edible, making this squash very easy to cook with. The air fryer caramelizes the outside of the squash, making it even sweeter in this recipe than when cooking it in a conventional oven.

2 medium Delicata squash, ends trimmed, halved lengthwise, seeded, cut into ½-inch half moons

2 shallots, chopped

2 garlic cloves, crushed

Avocado oil cooking spray

¼ cup grated Parmesan cheese

1 teaspoon red pepper flakes

¼ cup pumpkin seeds

⅓ cup balsamic vinegar

1. Preheat the air fryer to 400°F.

2. Working in batches, place the squash, shallots, and garlic in the air fryer basket in a single layer. Mist with the avocado oil and season with the Parmesan cheese and red pepper flakes. Cook for 10 minutes, then stir or shake the vegetables. Top with the pumpkin seeds and continue to cook for 5 minutes, until the timer goes off and the squash is golden brown.

3. When done, transfer the vegetables to a bowl and drizzle with the balsamic vinegar.

Per serving: Calories: 137; Total fat: 5g; Saturated fat: 2g; Cholesterol: 5g; Sodium: 120mg; Carbohydrates: 20g; Fiber: 2g; Protein: 6g

Fried Cauliflower Bites with Buffalo Sauce

Serves 4 / **Prep time:** 10 minutes / **Cook time:** 5 minutes / **Temperature:** 370°F

30-MINUTE, VEGAN

I created this recipe to give you a delicious, crispy cauliflower bite that tastes like it was fried. The Buffalo sauce is tahini-based, guaranteeing a creamy dip without using butter; I recommend Cholula brand hot sauce, but if you cannot find it, find one with less than 100 mg sodium per teaspoon.

For the cauliflower bites

1 cup unsweetened almond milk

1 tablespoon cornstarch or arrowroot powder

1½ cups whole wheat panko bread crumbs

2 tablespoons dried basil

1 tablespoon paprika

1 tablespoon granulated garlic

Pinch sea salt

12 ounces cauliflower florets

Extra-virgin olive oil cooking spray

For the sauce

¼ cup no-added-salt tahini

4 teaspoons hot sauce, such as Cholula

2 teaspoons apple cider vinegar

1 teaspoon smoked paprika

2½ tablespoons water

To make the cauliflower bites

1. Preheat the air fryer to 370°F.

2. In a small bowl, whisk together the almond milk and cornstarch.

3. In another small bowl, stir together the panko bread crumbs, basil, paprika, garlic, and salt.

4. One at a time, dunk each cauliflower floret into the almond milk mixture and then coat in the panko bread crumb mixture. Repeat until all the florets are coated.

5. Working in batches if necessary, arrange the cauliflower bites in a single layer in the air fryer basket, mist with the olive oil, and cook for 6 minutes. The cauliflower bites are done when golden brown.

To make the sauce

6. While the cauliflower is cooking, in a medium bowl, whisk together the tahini, hot sauce, vinegar, and paprika. Whisk in the water, 1 tablespoon at a time, until the consistency is smooth but pourable.

7. Serve the cauliflower bites with the Buffalo sauce on the side.

Per serving: Calories: 262; Total fat: 11g; Saturated fat: 2g; Cholesterol: 0g; Sodium: 230mg; Carbohydrates: 33g; Fiber: 7g; Protein: 10g

Crispy Ginger Edamame

Serves 4 / **Prep time:** 5 minutes / **Cook time:** 10 minutes / **Temperature:** 375°F

30-MINUTE, GLUTEN-FREE, VEGAN

Edamame are immature soybeans, and they easily take on any spice used in recipes. Beans are high in fiber and protein and low in fat, making them a nutritious snack. This recipe is great for an on-the-go snack when you feel like having something crunchy. Coconut aminos are a great low-sodium substitute for soy sauce and can usually be found in the health or natural food aisle of your supermarket.

2 cups shelled frozen edamame, thawed

2 tablespoons coconut aminos

2 teaspoons freshly grated ginger

2 tablespoons sesame seeds

2 tablespoons hemp seeds

2 tablespoons extra-virgin olive oil

1. Preheat the air fryer to 375°F.

2. Place the edamame in a medium bowl.

3. In a small bowl, whisk together the coconut aminos, ginger, sesame seeds, hemp seeds, and olive oil.

4. Sprinkle half of the coconut amino mixture over the edamame and toss to coat.

5. Working in batches if necessary, arrange the edamame in a single layer in the air fryer basket and cook for 8 minutes, shaking or stirring frequently.

6. Once done, transfer the edamame to a medium bowl, sprinkle with the remaining coconut aminos mixture, and toss to coat.

VARIATION TIP: Cooked chickpeas or cannellini beans (drained, if canned) also work great in the air fryer. Season with paprika instead of ginger for a new flavor profile. The cooking time and temperature will be the same.

Per serving: Calories: 243; Total fat: 16g; Saturated fat: 2g; Cholesterol: 0g; Sodium: 178mg; Carbohydrates: 12g; Fiber: 5g; Protein: 11g

Snap Pea Chips with Sesame Seeds

Serves 3 / **Prep time:** 5 minutes / **Cook time:** 10 minutes / **Temperature:** 375°F

30-MINUTE, GLUTEN-FREE, VEGAN

Snap peas, also known as sugar snap peas, have an edible outer pod and a fresh, sweet flavor that requires very little seasoning. Sesame seeds contain important minerals such as calcium, magnesium, and zinc and are used here to season the peas. This recipe is very simple to make and is a terrific side dish, addition to a salad, or even a vehicle for a dip such as hummus.

24 ounces fresh snap peas

Extra-virgin olive oil cooking spray

1 teaspoon sweet paprika

2 tablespoons sesame seeds

¼ teaspoon sea salt

1. Preheat the air fryer to 375°F.

2. Working in batches if necessary, arrange the snap peas in a single layer in the air fryer basket. Mist with the olive oil and season with the paprika, sesame seeds, and salt. Cook for 8 minutes, shaking the basket halfway through the cooking time.

3. Remove the peas from the basket and allow to cool before eating.

AIR-FRYER TIP: The cooking time suggested here will brown the outside of the snap peas a little bit; if you prefer a softer snap pea, cook it for a little less time. I recommend using fresh snap peas for this recipe, as frozen ones tend to get a little soggy.

Per serving: Calories: 120; Total fat: 4g; Saturated fat: 1g; Cholesterol: 0g; Sodium: 207mg; Carbohydrates: 13g; Fiber: 1g; Protein: 9g

Chewy Date Bars

Makes 4 bars / **Prep time:** 10 minutes / **Cook time:** 10 minutes / **Temperature:** 320°F

30-MINUTE, GLUTEN-FREE, VEGAN

Homemade bars are great for on-the-go snacks or when you're craving something sweet. This recipe uses Medjool dates as a natural sweetener, so you don't have to load up on added sugars. Fun fact: By weight, Medjool dates contain 50 percent more potassium than bananas! The oats, nuts, and seeds all provide fiber, giving this bar 7 grams of fiber per serving—leftovers will last for up to 1 week in an airtight container.

½ cup raw cashews

¼ cup unsalted natural peanut butter

½ cup gluten-free old-fashioned rolled oats

2 tablespoons chia seeds

5 Medjool dates, pitted

2 tablespoons almond milk

1 teaspoon ground cinnamon

½ teaspoon ground nutmeg

¼ teaspoon ground cloves

¼ teaspoon sea salt

1. In a high-speed blender or food processor, combine the cashews, peanut butter, oats, chia seeds, dates, almond milk, cinnamon, nutmeg, cloves, and salt. Pulse on high speed until the ingredients are well combined and the dough starts to come together.

2. Line the air fryer basket or an air fryer baking pan with parchment paper. Pour the batter into the bottom, pressing it firmly down with your fingers to form an even layer. Set the temperature to 320°F and cook for 8 minutes, until golden brown on top.

3. Allow to cool completely, then cut into 2-inch-thick bars.

VARIATION TIP: Feel free to switch up the nut butter in this recipe; cashew butter or almond butter could be good replacements for the peanut butter.

Per serving (1 bar): Calories: 337; Total fat: 18g; Saturated fat: 3g; Cholesterol: 0g; Sodium: 159mg; Carbohydrates: 41g; Fiber: 7g; Protein: 9g

Lemon-Herb Roasted Almonds

Serves 4 / **Prep time:** 5 minutes / **Cook time:** 5 minutes / **Temperature:** 350°F

30-MINUTE, GLUTEN-FREE, VEGAN

In general, all nut types are a healthy snack, and almonds are a plant-based calcium powerhouse. Roasted and salted store-bought nuts are not the best option when you're following the DASH diet, however. Instead, buy plain nuts and roast them yourself with your choice of herbs. This way, you can control the sodium levels while adding your favorite flavors. This recipe is delicious alone or tossed in a salad.

1½ cups raw sliced almonds

Extra-virgin olive oil cooking spray

2 tablespoons finely chopped fresh rosemary

2 tablespoons grated lemon zest

¼ teaspoon sea salt

1. Preheat the air fryer to 350°F.

2. In a medium bowl, mist the almonds with the olive oil. Add the rosemary, lemon zest, and salt and toss to combine.

3. Working in batches if necessary, place the almonds in a single layer in the air fryer basket and cook for 6 minutes, shaking the basket or stirring the contents a few times during the cooking time.

VARIATION TIP: Try a spicy version by replacing the lemon and rosemary with cayenne pepper and cumin. Or try making a sweet version using cinnamon and coconut sugar.

Per serving: Calories: 285; Total fat: 24g; Saturated fat: 2g; Cholesterol: 0g; Sodium: 147mg; Carbohydrates: 11g; Fiber: 7g; Protein: 10g

Onion and Garlic Roasted Bell Peppers

Serves 4 / **Prep time:** 10 minutes / **Cook time:** 15 minutes / **Temperature:** 350°F

30-MINUTE, GLUTEN-FREE

Roasted onions and bell peppers are very versatile. They can be used in antipasto platters, in salads, or as a take on a Mexican-inspired flavor for fajitas. The air fryer makes roasting onions and bell peppers a breeze and brings out the sweetness of the Vidalia onion. I suggest making a batch of this and having it on hand to add to other meals easily.

4 large red bell peppers, seeded and sliced

½ cup sliced sweet Vidalia onion

2 garlic cloves, crushed

Extra-virgin olive oil cooking spray

¼ cup pine nuts

6 tablespoons grated Parmesan cheese

1. In a medium bowl, stir together the peppers, onion, and garlic and spray with the olive oil.

2. Working in batches if necessary, spread the vegetables out in the air fryer basket. They can overlap. Set the temperature to 350°F and cook for 15 minutes, shaking the basket or stirring the contents throughout the cooking time. Five minutes before the end of the cook time, add the pine nuts and shake the basket.

3. Remove from the basket and sprinkle with the Parmesan cheese.

Per serving: Calories: 153; Total fat: 8g; Saturated fat: 2g; Cholesterol: 8g; Sodium: 183mg; Carbohydrates: 17g; Fiber: 5g; Protein: 6g

Banana and Apple Chips with Peanut Butter–Yogurt Dip

Serves 4 / **Prep time:** 5 minutes / **Cook time:** 10 minutes / **Temperature:** 350°F

30-MINUTE, GLUTEN-FREE, VEGETARIAN

Banana and apple chips are sweet and healthy snacks, and they are amazing when made in the air fryer. This recipe is so simple and highlights the delicious flavors of the fruits—you'll never be tempted to buy premade again. The dip is quick and easy to whip up, giving you a satisfying snack in a mere 15 minutes.

2 medium bananas, cut into ¼-inch slices

2 medium apples, cored, cut into ¼-inch slices

2 teaspoons ground cinnamon

1½ cups plain low-fat Greek yogurt

2 tablespoons unsalted natural peanut butter

1. Working in batches if necessary, lay the banana and apple slices in a single layer in the air fryer basket and season with the cinnamon. Set the air fryer temperature to 350°F and cook for 10 minutes, flipping the fruit halfway through the cooking time.

2. While the fruit is cooking, in a small bowl, stir together the yogurt and peanut butter until well combined. Serve the fruit chips immediately with the yogurt dip.

VARIATION TIP: If mangos are in season, use a firm mango and slice it thinly to create a mango chip.

Per serving: Calories: 207; Total fat: 5g; Saturated fat: 1g; Cholesterol: 5g; Sodium: 36mg; Carbohydrates: 33g; Fiber: 5g; Protein: 12g

Blueberry Pie Rice Cakes

Makes 4 rice cakes / **Prep time:** 5 minutes / **Cook time:** 5 minutes / **Temperature:** 375°F

30-MINUTE, GLUTEN-FREE, VEGAN

Blueberry pie is my childhood favorite dessert, and the warm blueberries in this filling treat bring back great memories of family gatherings. I transformed this dessert into a simple healthy snack that can be created in only 10 minutes. You will notice that the heat from the air fryer will cause some of the blueberries to burst, releasing their delicious juices.

4 low-sodium rice cakes

8 tablespoons
  almond butter

2½ cups blueberries

1. Assemble the rice cakes by spreading each one with 2 tablespoons of almond butter, then topping each with one-quarter of the blueberries.

2. Working in batches if necessary, place the rice cakes in a single layer in the air fryer basket. Set the temperature to 375°F and cook for 5 minutes, checking them after 3 minutes, until the blueberries are blistering. These treats are best served warm.

VARIATION TIP: Frozen blueberries can be swapped for fresh blueberries. Try frozen wild blueberries to increase the sweetness.

Per serving (1 rice cake): Calories: 315; Total fat: 18g; Saturated fat: 1g; Cholesterol: 0g; Sodium: 33mg; Carbohydrates: 35g; Fiber: 6g; Protein: 8g

Plant-Based

Protein Fried Gnocchi with Pesto

Serves 4 / **Prep time:** 20 minutes / **Cook time:** 10 minutes / **Temperature:** 375°F

30-MINUTE, GLUTEN-FREE, VEGAN

This gnocchi dish doubles down on nutritious ingredients by replacing a potato base with a combination of cauliflower and chickpea flour. It's a great way to get in an extra serving of vegetables, and the chickpea flour adds plant-based protein. Cooking the gnocchi in the air fryer results in a nice toasty exterior, perfect for holding the accompanying pesto sauce. These are best if eaten the same day, although you can freeze cut gnocchi dough until ready to cook, then proceed from step 6.

For the gnocchi

2 (16-ounce) bags riced cauliflower (thawed, if frozen)

1½ cups chickpea flour

¼ teaspoon sea salt

2 tablespoons brown rice flour

Extra-virgin olive oil cooking spray

To make the gnocchi

1. Spread the cauliflower rice in a single layer in the air fryer basket. Set the temperature to 375°F and cook for 5 minutes.

2. Remove the cauliflower rice from the basket and allow to cool to room temperature. Transfer it to a paper towel or dishcloth and squeeze out any excess moisture.

3. Continue to heat the air fryer at 375°F until ready to cook the gnocchi.

4. In a food processor or high-speed blender, process the cauliflower rice, chickpea flour, and salt until the ingredients are well combined and form a sticky dough, about 30 seconds.

5. Lay a piece of parchment paper on the counter, dust it with the rice flour, and place the dough on top. Cut into 4 wedges. Roll each wedge into a rope over the flour. Cut each rope into 1-inch gnocchi pieces.

6. Working in batches if necessary, place the gnocchi in the air fryer basket, mist with the olive oil, and cook for 5 minutes, or until golden brown.

For the pesto

1 bunch fresh
 basil, stemmed

3 tablespoons extra-virgin
 olive oil

1 garlic clove

½ cup pine nuts

1 tablespoon freshly
 squeezed lemon juice

¼ teaspoon sea salt

2 tablespoons water

Freshly ground
 black pepper

To make the pesto

7. While the gnocchi are cooking, in a high-speed blender or food processor, combine the basil, olive oil, garlic, pine nuts, lemon juice, and salt and blend on high speed until well mixed. If the mixture appears dry, add the water, 1 teaspoon at a time. Season with pepper to taste.

8. Serve the gnocchi topped with the pesto.

VARIATION TIP: Try these versatile dumplings with a marinara or butternut squash sauce.

Per serving: Calories: 407; Total fat: 23g; Saturated fat: 3g; Cholesterol: 0g; Sodium: 369mg; Carbohydrates: 39g; Fiber: 12g; Protein: 13g

Crispy Balsamic Eggplant, Tomato, and Mozzarella Stacks

Serves 4 / **Prep time:** 10 minutes / **Cook time:** 15 minutes / **Temperature:** 390°F, then 250°F

30-MINUTE, VEGETARIAN

In my house, this recipe is typically made in the summer months on the grill, but with the air fryer, this recipe can be made throughout the year, no grill needed! I added a twist by coating the eggplant in panko bread crumbs for a crunchy bite. Serve over a bed of greens for a complete meal.

1 large eggplant, cut into ½-inch-thick rounds

¼ cup balsamic vinegar

2 tablespoons extra-virgin olive oil

1 tablespoon granulated garlic

1 tablespoon dried basil

1 tablespoon dried oregano

1 teaspoon red pepper flakes

1 cup whole wheat panko bread crumbs

2 beefsteak tomatoes, cut into ½-inch-thick rounds

4 ounces part-skim mozzarella cheese, cut into ½-inch-thick rounds

1. Preheat the air fryer to 390°F.

2. In a large bowl, toss the eggplant with the vinegar, olive oil, garlic, basil, oregano, and red pepper flakes.

3. Remove an eggplant slice from the balsamic mixture and coat in the panko bread crumbs, pressing the panko bread crumbs firmly into the eggplant. Set aside. Repeat until all the eggplant slices are coated.

4. Add the tomato slices to the bowl with the balsamic mixture and set aside to marinate.

5. Working in batches if necessary, place the eggplant slices in the air fryer basket in a single layer and cook for 8 minutes, or until golden brown.

6. Remove the eggplant. Make the stacks in this order, from the base up: eggplant, tomato, eggplant, tomato, eggplant, and top with a slice of mozzarella cheese.

7. Working in batches if necessary, place the stacks in the air fryer. Set the temperature to 250°F and cook for 5 minutes.

VARIATION TIP: To make the stacks gluten-free, use gluten-free panko bread crumbs.

AIR-FRYER TIP: Ensure the eggplant is sliced evenly to prevent overcooking or burning.

Per serving: Calories: 325; Total fat: 17g; Saturated fat: 5g; Cholesterol: 18g; Sodium: 269mg; Carbohydrates: 32g; Fiber: 8g; Protein: 13g

Zucchini Fritters with Corn Salsa

Serves 4 / **Prep time:** 10 minutes, plus 30 minutes to rest / **Cook time:** 10 minutes / **Temperature:** 370°F

DAIRY-FREE, GLUTEN-FREE, VEGETARIAN

Fritters are little patties that are typically deep-fried, which can be messy, smelly, and not DASH compliant. Using the air fryer is easier, and there's no smoky oil smell or splashing oil. Plus, the air fryer will save you a ton of calories while still giving you the crispy texture you love in fritters. The salsa topping in this recipe adds a fresh taste.

For the salsa

2 cups cherry tomatoes, diced, juices reserved

1 shallot, diced

1 cup corn kernels (thawed, if frozen)

½ cup chopped fresh cilantro

1 tablespoon freshly squeezed lime juice

1 tablespoon extra-virgin olive oil

Freshly ground black pepper

For the fritters

2 large zucchini, coarsely grated (about 4 cups)

1 (15-ounce) can low-sodium cannellini beans, rinsed and drained

2 large egg whites

3 tablespoons chopped fresh parsley

2 garlic cloves, minced

¼ teaspoon sea salt

½ cup almond flour

To make the salsa

1. In a medium bowl, stir together the tomatoes, shallot, corn, cilantro, lime juice, and olive oil. Season with pepper to taste. Allow to sit for at least 30 minutes at room temperature or in the refrigerator to allow the flavors to meld.

To make the fritters

2. Preheat the air fryer to 370°F.

3. Using a dish towel or paper towel, pat the grated zucchini dry to remove any excess water.

4. In a large bowl, use a fork to combine the zucchini, beans, egg whites, parsley, garlic, salt, and almond flour. Slightly mash the beans while mixing. Using damp hands, form the zucchini mixture into 16 patties.

5. Working in batches if necessary, place the patties in a single layer in the air fryer basket and cook for 12 minutes, until golden brown. Serve the fritters topped with salsa.

Per serving: Calories: 288; Total fat: 12g; Saturated fat: 1g; Cholesterol: 0g; Sodium: 236mg; Carbohydrates: 35g; Fiber: 10g; Protein: 14g

Zucchini Lasagna Roll-Ups

Serves 4 / **Prep time:** 20 minutes / **Cook time:** 10 minutes / **Temperature:** 400°F

30-MINUTE, VEGETARIAN

For this variation on lasagna, I transformed a layered, oven-baked lasagna into individual roll-ups that cook quickly in the air fryer but provide the same great flavors. Plus, unlike traditional lasagnas, the panko breadcrumbs and the use of the air fryer ensures each roll-up has a crunchy bite. Using mashed beans instead of beef provides protein and extra fiber. Using zucchini in place of lasagna noodles offers a healthy, low-carb alternative. Enjoy leftovers by quickly heating in the air fryer for a couple minutes before serving.

2 cups part-skim ricotta cheese

½ cup low-sodium cannellini beans, drained, rinsed, and mashed

2 cups fresh spinach

2 tablespoons granulated garlic, divided

2 tablespoons dried basil, divided

2 tablespoons dried oregano, divided

2 teaspoons freshly ground black pepper, divided

2 large zucchini, cut lengthwise into ⅛-inch-thick strips

2 cups unsweetened almond milk

1 tablespoon extra-virgin olive oil

1 cup whole wheat panko bread crumbs

Extra-virgin olive oil cooking spray

2 cups low-sodium marinara sauce

1. Preheat the air fryer to 400°F.

2. In a medium bowl, stir together the ricotta cheese, mashed beans, spinach, 1 tablespoon of garlic powder, 1 tablespoon of basil, 1 tablespoon of oregano, and 1 teaspoon of pepper.

3. Lay the zucchini slices flat in a single layer. Spread 1 tablespoon of the ricotta mixture along each zucchini slice. Roll up each slice and secure with a toothpick.

4. In a separate medium bowl, whisk together the almond milk and olive oil.

5. In a small bowl, stir together the panko bread crumbs with the remaining 1 tablespoon of garlic powder, 1 tablespoon of basil, 1 tablespoon of oregano, and 1 teaspoon of pepper.

6. One at a time, dunk each zucchini roll-up into the almond milk mixture and then coat in the panko bread crumb mixture. Repeat until all are coated.

7. Working in batches if necessary, place each zucchini roll-up in the air fryer basket in a single layer, mist with the olive oil, and cook for 10 minutes.

8. While the zucchini roll-ups are cooking, heat the marinara sauce on the stovetop over medium heat until warm. Serve the zucchini roll-ups topped with marinara sauce.

VARIATION TIP: To make this recipe vegan, replace the ricotta with a nondairy ricotta cheese; just be sure to check the sodium content. To make it gluten-free, use gluten-free panko bread crumbs.

Per serving: Calories: 338; Total fat: 13g; Saturated fat: 3g; Cholesterol: 20g; Sodium: 370mg; Carbohydrates: 40g; Fiber: 7g; Protein: 19g

Toasted Chickpea-Quinoa Bowl

Serves 4 / **Prep time:** 10 minutes / **Cook time:** 10 minutes / **Temperature:** 350°F

30-MINUTE, GLUTEN-FREE, VEGAN

This is my rendition of a vegan power bowl. Power bowls are quick and easy meals with balanced amounts of protein, carbohydrates, and healthy fats to leave you feeling energized and satisfied. This recipe is loaded with nutrient-dense food, providing many micronutrients (vitamins and minerals). Meal prep this recipe for several days and forget about sad lunches!

For the vinaigrette

2 tablespoons freshly squeezed lemon juice

2 tablespoons extra-virgin olive oil

1 tablespoon white wine vinegar

1 tablespoon Italian seasoning

1 teaspoon Dijon mustard

1 teaspoon freshly ground black pepper

For the chickpea-quinoa bowl

1 (15-ounce) can low-sodium chickpeas, drained and rinsed

2 large zucchini, chopped

3 cups coarsely chopped cauliflower florets

1 tablespoon extra-virgin olive oil

1 teaspoon paprika

1 teaspoon garlic powder

1 teaspoon ground cumin

½ cup dry quinoa

4 cups fresh arugula

To make the vinaigrette

1. In a small bowl, whisk together the lemon juice, olive oil, and vinegar. Add the Italian seasoning, mustard, and black pepper and whisk again.

To make the chickpea-quinoa bowl

2. In a medium bowl, stir together the chickpeas, zucchini, cauliflower, olive oil, paprika, garlic powder, and cumin.

3. Working in batches if necessary, place the chickpea and vegetable mixture in the air fryer basket in a single layer. Set the temperature to 350°F and cook for 4 minutes. Shake or stir and cook for 4 minutes, until the vegetables are tender.

4. Cook the quinoa according to the package directions.

5. To assemble, divide the quinoa and arugula between bowls, top with the chickpeas and vegetables, and drizzle with the vinaigrette.

SUBSTITUTION TIP: You can switch up the cooked vegetables in this recipe; eggplant or Brussels sprouts would work great. Eggplant would require the same cook time, but if using Brussels sprouts, cook them for an additional 15 minutes.

Per serving: Calories: 369; Total fat: 15g; Saturated fat: 2g; Cholesterol: 0g; Sodium: 295mg; Carbohydrates: 48g; Fiber: 12g; Protein: 14g

Fried Pasta Chips with Tomato-Basil Dip

Serves 4 / **Prep time:** 20 minutes / **Cook time:** 15 minutes / **Temperature:** 375°F

GLUTEN-FREE, VEGAN

This crunchy pasta dish is a textural delight because the noodles get crisped up like chips in the air fryer. This recipe uses chickpea pasta, which is high in protein—about 13 grams per serving, compared to only 1 gram in traditional wheat-based pastas. Choose your favorite short pasta shape, such as bow ties or rigatoni, for easy dipping.

For the tomato-basil dip

1 bunch fresh basil, stemmed

1 tablespoon extra-virgin olive oil

1 garlic clove

½ cup pine nuts

1 tablespoon freshly squeezed lemon juice

¼ cup cherry tomatoes

¼ teaspoon sea salt

1 to 2 teaspoons water (optional)

Freshly ground black pepper

For the pasta chips

12 ounces chickpea pasta

2 tablespoons extra-virgin olive oil

4 tablespoons nutritional yeast

1 teaspoon dried basil

1 teaspoon dried oregano

1 teaspoon granulated garlic

½ teaspoon sea salt

To make the tomato-basil dip

1. In a high-speed blender or food processor, combine the basil, olive oil, garlic, pine nuts, lemon juice, tomatoes, and salt and blend on high speed until well mixed. If the mixture appears dry, add the water. Season with pepper to taste.

To make the pasta chips

2. Preheat the air fryer to 375°F.

3. Bring a large pot of water to a boil. Cook the pasta at a boil, stirring occasionally, until al dente, about 8 minutes.

4. Transfer the pasta to a large bowl and drizzle with the olive oil. Stir in the nutritional yeast, basil, oregano, garlic, and salt.

5. Working in batches if necessary, place the pasta in the air fryer basket in a single layer and cook for 5 minutes. Shake or stir when the timer goes off, then continue to cook for another 2 to 3 minutes, until the pasta is golden brown.

6. Transfer to a paper-towel–lined plate and allow to cool before serving alongside the tomato-basil dip.

Per serving: Calories: 499; Total fat: 20g; Saturated fat: 3g; Cholesterol: 0g; Sodium: 303mg; Carbohydrates: 57g; Fiber: 12g; Protein: 23g

Penne with Sizzling Tomatoes and Artichokes

Serves 4 / **Prep time:** 20 minutes / **Cook time:** 10 minutes / **Temperature:** 375°F

30-MINUTE, GLUTEN-FREE, VEGAN

This recipe is simple but packed with flavor. The sauce is created by air frying tomatoes and artichoke hearts. The air fryer gives the tomatoes a delicious char and causes them to burst and give up their juices to make a light sauce. The easy cleanup is always a plus on busy days.

12 ounces chickpea penne

4 cups cherry tomatoes

1 (7-ounce) jar marinated artichoke hearts, drained and chopped

2 tablespoons extra-virgin olive oil

1 tablespoon dried basil

1 tablespoon dried oregano

2 teaspoons granulated garlic

1. Preheat the air fryer to 375°F. Cook the pasta according to the package directions.

2. In a large bowl, stir together the tomatoes, artichoke hearts, olive oil, basil, oregano, and garlic.

3. Line the air fryer basket with parchment paper or use an air fryer baking pan. Working in batches if necessary, place the tomatoes and artichokes into the prepared basket and cook for 10 minutes, until the tomatoes start to blister and pop.

4. When the tomatoes and artichokes are done, toss with the pasta and serve immediately.

AIR-FRYER TIP: It is important to line the air fryer basket or use the pan for this recipe to retain any of the tomato juices that come out during cooking—this is the sauce for your pasta.

Per serving: Calories: 468; Total fat: 16g; Saturated fat: 2g; Cholesterol: 0g; Sodium: 204mg; Carbohydrates: 62g; Fiber: 13g; Protein: 21g

Black Bean Bake with Avocado

Serves 4 / **Prep time:** 10 minutes / **Cook time:** 10 minutes / **Temperature:** 375°F

30-MINUTE, GLUTEN-FREE, VEGAN

This easy dish of baked black beans is ready in well under 30 minutes, making it perfect for busy weeknights. The recipe combines beans, corn, vegetables, and avocado for a hearty meal that even a meat eater will love. Serve this dish with some mini bell peppers for scooping, or try using some no-salt-added tortilla chips.

1 (15-ounce) can low-sodium black beans, rinsed and drained

2 cups corn kernels (thawed, if frozen)

2 large bell peppers, diced

½ cup chopped red onion

1 garlic clove, minced

2 tablespoons extra-virgin olive oil

1 tablespoon freshly squeezed lime juice

2 teaspoons chili powder

2 teaspoons ground cumin

½ teaspoon paprika

¼ teaspoon dried onion granules

¼ teaspoon dried oregano

1 teaspoon freshly ground black pepper

3 tablespoons nutritional yeast

1 cup chopped fresh cilantro, for garnish

1 Hass avocado, sliced

1. Preheat the air fryer to 375°F.

2. In a large bowl, stir together the black beans, corn, bell peppers, onion, garlic, olive oil, lime juice, chili powder, cumin, paprika, onion, oregano, and pepper.

3. Working in batches if necessary, spread the bean mixture in an air fryer baking pan and place the pan in the air fryer basket. Cook for 6 minutes.

4. After the timer goes off, sprinkle the mixture with the nutritional yeast and cook for another 3 minutes, or until the top is golden brown.

5. To serve, remove from the pan, garnish with the cilantro, and top with the avocado slices.

VARIATION TIP: You can substitute ½ cup of shredded low-sodium cheddar for the nutritional yeast in this recipe.

Per serving: Calories: 393; Total fat: 14g; Saturated fat: 2g; Cholesterol: 0g; Sodium: 12mg; Carbohydrates: 58g; Fiber: 20g; Protein: 16g

Falafel with Mint-Tahini Sauce

Serves 4 / **Prep time:** 15 minutes, plus overnight to soak / **Cook time:** 10 minutes / **Temperature:** 350°F

GLUTEN-FREE, VEGAN

This recipe uses the convection cooking magic of the air fryer to create perfectly cooked falafel—all tender middles and crispy outer shells—without the mess of deep-frying. I top them with a tahini dressing spiked with mint for a cool, creamy accompaniment. This recipe is terrific for meal prep. Make an extra batch and use the falafel all week in in salads, power bowls, or wraps.

For the falafel

1 cup dried chickpeas, soaked overnight, drained, rinsed, and patted dry

½ red onion, chopped

½ red bell pepper, chopped

½ cup fresh parsley, stemmed

½ cup chopped fresh mint

1 teaspoon ground cumin

2 garlic cloves, minced

¼ teaspoon dried oregano

¼ teaspoon sea salt

1 teaspoon extra-virgin olive oil

For the mint-tahini sauce

½ cup tahini

½ cup chopped fresh mint

2 tablespoons freshly squeezed lemon juice

¼ teaspoon sea salt

3 tablespoons water (optional)

To make the falafel

1. Preheat the air fryer to 350°F.

2. In a food processor bowl, combine the chickpeas, onion, bell pepper, parsley, mint, cumin, garlic, oregano, salt, and olive oil. Pulse, scraping down the bowl occasionally, until well combined into a rough paste.

3. Using damp hands, divide the falafel mixture into 10 patties, about 1 inch thick.

4. Working in batches if necessary, place the patties in a single layer in the air fryer basket. Set the temperature to 350°F and cook for 8 minutes, flipping halfway through, or until golden brown.

To make the mint-tahini sauce

5. While the falafel is cooking, in a medium bowl, stir together the tahini, mint, lemon juice, and salt until smooth. If the sauce is thick, add the water, 1 tablespoon at a time, until it reaches a consistency thin enough for dipping.

6. Serve the warm falafel with the mint-tahini sauce.

Per serving: Calories: 398; Total fat: 21g; Saturated fat: 3g; Cholesterol: 0g; Sodium: 338mg; Carbohydrates: 45g; Fiber: 13g; Protein: 17g

Quinoa-Lentil Burgers

Makes 4 burgers / **Prep time:** 20 minutes, plus 30 minutes to chill / **Cook time:** 10 minutes
Temperature: 350°F

GLUTEN-FREE, VEGAN

These burgers are a great option for plant-based individuals, but also for anyone looking for a low-fat protein source. They are loaded with fiber and make a hearty and satisfying meal. Serve these patties with a whole wheat bun and sliced avocado, or ditch the bread and eat them over a large green salad. I love using the air fryer for burgers to cut down on cooking time and for easy cleanup.

⅓ cup dry quinoa

1 cup dried red lentils

4 cups water

4 cups spinach

2 ounces (12 to 15) sun-dried tomatoes, chopped

½ large red onion, chopped

½ cup almond flour

¼ teaspoon granulated garlic

¼ teaspoon ground cumin

1. In a medium saucepan, combine the quinoa and lentils with the water. Bring to a boil, then reduce the heat, cover, and simmer until the quinoa and lentils are cooked through, about 15 minutes. In the last minute of cooking, add the spinach and let wilt.

2. Drain the quinoa mixture and transfer to a large bowl. Stir in the sun-dried tomatoes, onion, almond flour, garlic, and cumin then cover and refrigerate for at least 30 minutes or up to overnight.

3. Preheat the air fryer to 350°F.

4. Divide the burger mixture into 4 large patties, about 5 inches in diameter.

5. Working in batches if necessary, place the burgers in a single layer in the air fryer basket and cook for 10 minutes. Flip the burgers over and cook for another 2 minutes, or until golden brown. Serve immediately over salad or in a whole wheat bun.

VARIATION TIP: Whole wheat flour can be replaced with almond flour in an equal amount.

Per serving (1 burger): Calories: 291; Total fat: 10g; Saturated fat: 1g; Cholesterol: 0g; Sodium: 130mg; Carbohydrates: 38g; Fiber: 7g; Protein: 13g

Eggplant Bites with Marinara

Serves 4 / **Prep time:** 20 minutes / **Cook time:** 10 minutes / **Temperature:** 370°F

30-MINUTE, VEGAN

This recipe is a twist on the classic eggplant Parmesan, swapping out the cheese for nutritional yeast, which is considered a superfood for vegans because it contains all essential amino acids, making it a complete protein source. Compared to frying with oil, the air fryer slashes the calories in this classic. Homemade marinara sauce allows you to control your sodium intake and still have the dish ready in just 10 minutes.

For the marinara sauce

1 tablespoon extra-virgin olive oil

2 garlic cloves, minced

1 (15-ounce) can crushed tomatoes

1 tablespoon dried oregano

1 tablespoon dried basil

½ teaspoon freshly ground black pepper

½ teaspoon dried parsley

To make the marinara sauce

1. In a medium saucepan over medium-low heat, heat the olive oil, then add the garlic and sauté for 1 to 2 minutes, until fragrant.

2. Add the tomatoes, oregano, basil, pepper, and parsley. Simmer for 8 minutes, or until the sauce starts to bubble, stirring occasionally. Keep warm until ready to use.

For the eggplant bites

1 medium eggplant, peeled and cut into cubes

1 cup unsweetened almond milk

1 tablespoon extra-virgin olive oil

2 cups whole wheat panko bread crumbs

¼ cup nutritional yeast, plus more for sprinkling

1 tablespoon granulated garlic

1 tablespoon dried oregano

¼ teaspoon sea salt

Extra-virgin olive oil cooking spray

To make the eggplant bites

3. Preheat the air fryer to 370°F.

4. Place the eggplant on a paper towel or dishcloth and allow moisture to drain for about 5 minutes, then pat dry.

5. In a medium bowl, whisk together the almond milk and olive oil. In another medium bowl, stir together the panko bread crumbs, nutritional yeast, garlic, oregano, and salt.

6. One at a time, dunk the eggplant cubes into the almond milk mixture and then coat in the panko bread crumb mixture.

7. Working in batches if necessary, arrange the eggplant in a single layer in the air fryer basket. Mist with the olive oil and cook for 9 minutes, shaking or stirring halfway through.

8. After the timer goes off, sprinkle with additional nutritional yeast and cook for another 1 minute, until golden brown. Serve the eggplant bites with the marinara sauce on the side for dipping.

Per serving: Calories: 312; Total fat: 9g; Saturated fat: 1g; Cholesterol: 0g; Sodium: 434mg; Carbohydrates: 49g; Fiber: 12g; Protein: 13g

Tempeh Veggie Tacos

Serves 4 / **Prep time:** 10 minutes / **Cook time:** 10 minutes / **Temperature:** 325°F

30-MINUTE, GLUTEN-FREE, VEGAN

Tempeh is a fermented soy product and a popular replacement for meat. Tempeh is high in protein and many micronutrients, including magnesium and calcium. It has a chewy texture and slightly nutty flavor but easily holds on to flavor when seasoned with spices. Tempeh can be prepared in a variety of ways, but I especially love the crispy texture it gains with air frying.

12 ounces tempeh, cut into cubes

1 tablespoon chili powder

½ teaspoon paprika

½ teaspoon ground cumin

¼ teaspoon sea salt

1 tablespoon freshly squeezed lime juice

Extra-virgin olive oil cooking spray bottle

1 cup chopped romaine lettuce

8 (6-inch) corn tortillas

1 bell pepper, chopped

½ cup chopped fresh cilantro

1 medium Hass avocado

1 jalapeño, sliced (optional)

1. Preheat the air fryer to 325°F.

2. In a medium bowl, stir together the tempeh, chili powder, paprika, cumin, salt, and lime juice.

3. Working in batches if necessary, arrange the tempeh wedges in a single layer in the air fryer basket, being sure not to crowd them. Mist with the olive oil and cook for 10 minutes, or until the tempeh is browned and slightly crispy on the outside.

4. To assemble the tacos, layer the lettuce on the bottom of each tortilla. Top with the tempeh, bell pepper, cilantro, avocado, and jalapeño slices (if using).

VARIATION TIP: Firm beans, such as chickpeas, can be used in place of the tempeh; cook for the same time and at the same temperature.

Per serving (2 tacos): Calories: 360; Total fat: 17g; Saturated fat: 3g; Cholesterol: 0g; Sodium: 242mg; Carbohydrates: 39g; Fiber: 11g; Protein: 22g

Chickpea Frittata with Tomatoes and Watercress

Serves 4 / **Prep time:** 5 minutes / **Cook time:** 10 minutes / **Temperature:** 375°F

30-MINUTE, GLUTEN-FREE, VEGAN

This plant-based spin on a frittata is made without eggs. The chickpea flour provides a substantial amount of protein in this recipe, making it the same, if not more, than traditional frittatas; the baking powder in the batter makes it puff and crisp just like the eggy version. This meal is wonderful for breakfast, lunch, or dinner.

2 cups chickpea flour

3 tablespoons nutritional yeast

½ teaspoon baking powder

2 cups filtered water

¼ teaspoon sea salt

1 large bell pepper, chopped

12 ounces cherry tomatoes, chopped

2 cups chopped baby kale

Extra-virgin olive oil cooking spray

1 cup watercress or pea shoots

1. In a large bowl, whisk together the chickpea flour, nutritional yeast, baking powder, and water until smooth. Stir in the salt, bell pepper, tomatoes, and kale.

2. Working in batches if necessary, mist an air fryer baking pan with the olive oil, add the chickpea mixture, and smooth to an even layer. Place the pan in the air fryer basket and set the temperature to 375°F. Cook for 10 minutes, or until a toothpick inserted in the center comes out clean.

3. Top with the watercress and serve immediately.

VARIATION TIP: This recipe can be made in muffin tins for individual frittatas; just start checking for doneness after around 6 minutes.

Per serving: Calories: 226; Total fat: 4g; Saturated fat: 0g; Cholesterol: 0g; Sodium: 260mg; Carbohydrates: 35g; Fiber: 8g; Protein: 15g

Black Bean Burgers with Lettuce "Buns"

Makes 4 burgers / **Prep time:** 20 minutes / **Cook time:** 10 minutes / **Temperature:** 350°F

30-MINUTE, GLUTEN-FREE, VEGAN

Homemade burgers are easy to whip up on a busy weeknight and are quick to meal prep for the week, which is why there are two plant-based burgers in this cookbook. Black beans have almost double the fiber of lentils and a hearty texture. Lettuce wraps are a good low-carb, low-sodium alternative to buns. Pair this meal with Zucchini Chips (page 38) for a complete veggie-packed meal.

½ cup uncooked brown rice

3 cups canned low-sodium black beans, drained and rinsed

¼ cup brown rice flour

½ large red onion, chopped

1 large red bell pepper, diced

½ cup chopped fresh cilantro

1 teaspoon chili powder

1 teaspoon freshly ground black pepper

¼ teaspoon sea salt

1 medium Hass avocado, sliced

1 tomato, sliced

1 head Boston lettuce

1. Preheat the air fryer to 350°F. Cook the brown rice according to the package directions.

2. Mash the black beans in a large bowl until they are broken up, leaving some whole beans visible.

3. Stir in the brown rice, rice flour, onion, bell pepper, cilantro, chili powder, black pepper, and salt until evenly combined. Transfer to the refrigerator for 5 minutes to chill so that it is easier to form into patties.

4. Divide the bean mixture into 4 patties, about 5 inches in diameter.

5. Working in batches if necessary, place the burgers in a single layer in the air fryer basket and cook for 8 minutes. Flip them over and cook for another 2 minutes, or until golden brown.

6. To assemble, top each black bean patty with one-quarter of the avocado and tomato slices. Using 2 or 3 lettuce leaves per patty, wrap the leaves around the patty as tightly as you can.

VARIATION TIP: If you cannot locate Boston lettuce, romaine, red leaf, or iceberg lettuce would also work well.

Per serving (1 burger): Calories: 387; Total fat: 7g; Saturated fat: 1g; Cholesterol: 0g; Sodium: 176mg; Carbohydrates: 68g; Fiber: 19g; Protein: 15g

Roasted Apple–Butternut Squash Soup

Serves 4 / **Prep time:** 20 minutes / **Cook time:** 35 minutes / **Temperature:** 400°F

GLUTEN-FREE, VEGAN

Butternut squash soup typically includes saturated fats, such as cream or butter, as well as sugar. In this recipe, apples, carrots, and cinnamon provide the sweetness, while the sweet potato helps create an extra creamy texture without the added fat. Using the air fryer to roast the veggies will cut down on cooking time and provide easy cleanup.

2 cups peeled and cubed butternut squash

2 cups peeled and cubed sweet potato

1 cup peeled and chopped carrots

2 shallots, peeled and chopped

1 medium apple, cored and cut into 1-inch cubes

1 teaspoon ground cinnamon

Avocado oil cooking spray

3½ cups low-sodium vegetable broth

1. Preheat the air fryer to 400°F.

2. Working in batches if necessary, arrange the butternut squash, sweet potato, carrots, shallots, and apple in a single layer in the basket, being careful not to crowd them. Sprinkle with the cinnamon and mist with the avocado oil.

3. Cook the vegetables for 25 minutes, or until golden brown, shaking or stirring halfway through.

4. Carefully transfer the roasted vegetables to a 4-quart soup pot over medium heat. Add the broth and simmer for about 10 minutes.

5. Remove the soup from the heat and allow to cool slightly, then use an immersion blender or food processor to blend the vegetables until smooth.

Per serving: Calories: 287; Total fat: 0g; Saturated fat: 0g; Cholesterol: 0g; Sodium: 287mg; Carbohydrates: 69g; Fiber: 14g; Protein: 5g

Chapter 5

Poultry and Meat

Chicken Tenders with Avocado Dip

Serves 4 / **Prep time:** 10 minutes / **Cook time:** 10 minutes / **Temperature:** 400°F

30-MINUTE, GLUTEN-FREE

The air fryer guarantees crispy, crunchy, chicken tenders without excess oil. I frequently use almond flour in place of wheat flour because it contains four times more calcium. If you're looking for something to serve with this dish, I recommend Crispy Rosemary Parsnip Fries (page 34).

For the chicken tenders

1 cup unsweetened almond milk

2 large egg whites

½ cup almond flour

1 cup brown rice flour

1 tablespoon paprika

1 tablespoon granulated garlic

1 tablespoon dried oregano

¼ teaspoon sea salt

12 ounces chicken tenders

Extra-virgin olive oil cooking spray

For the dip

1 cup plain nonfat Greek yogurt

½ medium Hass avocado

1 teaspoon granulated garlic

1 teaspoon smoked paprika

½ teaspoon cayenne pepper

½ teaspoon freshly ground black pepper

½ teaspoon dried parsley

To make the chicken tenders

1. Preheat the air fryer to 400°F.

2. In a small bowl, whisk together the almond milk and egg whites. In another small bowl, stir together the almond flour, brown rice flour, paprika, granulated garlic, oregano, and salt.

3. One at a time, dunk each chicken tender into the almond milk mixture and then coat in the flour mixture.

4. Working in batches if necessary, arrange the chicken tenders in a single layer in the air fryer basket, being careful not to crowd them. Mist with the olive oil and cook for 10 minutes, flipping the tenders halfway through. The chicken is done when the internal temperature reaches 165°F.

To make the dip

5. While the chicken is cooking, in a small bowl, whisk together the yogurt, avocado, garlic, paprika, cayenne, black pepper, and parsley until smooth.

6. Serve the chicken tenders with the dipping sauce.

VARIATION TIP: To make this meal dairy-free, substitute non-dairy Greek yogurt. I like Kite Hill's almond milk Greek yogurt.

Per serving: Calories: 482; Total fat: 14g; Saturated fat: 2g; Cholesterol: 45g; Sodium: 415mg; Carbohydrates: 54g; Fiber: 13g; Protein: 42g

One-Basket Chicken with Lemon-Garlic Broccoli and Herbed Potatoes

Serves 4 / **Prep time:** 10 minutes / **Cook time:** 25 minutes / **Temperature:** 400°F

DAIRY-FREE, GLUTEN-FREE

My favorite meals are those that can be thrown together quickly in one basket and are still packed with flavor. Lemon pepper is delicious on chicken and is a great alternative to high-sodium spices and condiments. You can make your own lemon-pepper seasoning by combining dried lemon peel, black pepper, garlic, and onion powder—or purchase a store-bought version with no added salt. This one-basket meal is perfect for nights when you want to get a delicious meal on the table fast.

5 red potatoes, cubed (about 1 pound)

2 tablespoons dried rosemary

½ teaspoon red pepper flakes

¼ teaspoon sea salt

2 tablespoons avocado oil, divided

12 ounces skinless, boneless chicken thighs

2 tablespoons lemon-pepper seasoning

4 cups broccoli florets

3 tablespoons freshly squeezed lemon juice

1. Preheat the air fryer to 400°F.

2. In a large bowl, stir together the potatoes, rosemary, red pepper flakes, salt, and 1 tablespoon of avocado oil.

3. Working in batches if necessary, arrange the potatoes in a single layer in the air fryer basket and cook for 10 minutes.

4. While the potatoes are cooking, season the chicken with the lemon pepper. When the timer goes off, add the chicken thighs to the basket on top of the potatoes and set the timer for another 10 minutes.

5. When the timer goes off, add the broccoli to the basket on top of the chicken, drizzle with the lemon juice and remaining 1 tablespoon of avocado oil, and set the timer for another 5 minutes. The chicken is done when the internal temperature reaches 165°F.

Per serving: Calories: 314; Total fat: 11g; Saturated fat: 2g; Cholesterol: 68g; Sodium: 276mg; Carbohydrates: 34g; Fiber: 6g; Protein: 24g

Easy Juicy Meal Prep Chicken Breasts

Serves 4 / **Prep time:** 5 minutes, plus 5 minutes to rest / **Cook time:** 20 minutes / **Temperature:** 350°F

30-MINUTE, GLUTEN-FREE

I love this recipe because it's simple to prepare and yields tender, juicy chicken breasts in 20 minutes, cutting traditional cooking time by up to 30 percent. A great way to prepare for the week is to have proteins cooked and ready to be thrown into salads or rice bowls or served with a side of vegetables.

3 (6-ounce) boneless, skinless chicken breasts

1 tablespoon extra-virgin olive oil, plus more for misting

3 tablespoons Italian seasoning

½ teaspoon granulated garlic

¼ teaspoon sea salt

1 teaspoon freshly ground black pepper

¼ cup grated Parmesan cheese

1. Preheat the air fryer to 350°F.

2. In a large bowl, drizzle the chicken with the olive oil. Add the Italian seasoning, garlic, salt, and pepper. Rub the spices over all sides of the chicken breasts.

3. Working in batches if necessary, arrange the chicken breasts in a single layer in the air fryer basket. Mist with olive oil and cook for 20 minutes. The chicken is done when the internal temperature reaches 165°F.

4. When the timer goes off, transfer the chicken to a clean plate, sprinkle with the Parmesan cheese, and loosely cover with aluminum foil for 5 minutes.

AIR-FRYER TIP: Air fryer cooking times can vary, so check the chicken for doneness a few minutes before the timer goes off, to ensure it does not overcook. Be sure to use regular chicken breast, not thin cut, or the cooking time must be reduced.

Per serving: Calories: 285; Total fat: 11g; Saturated fat: 3g; Cholesterol: 114g; Sodium: 359mg; Carbohydrates: 3g; Fiber: 1g; Protein: 42g

Chicken Casserole with Spicy Brussels Sprouts and Potatoes

Serves 4 / **Prep time:** 5 minutes / **Cook time:** 15 minutes / **Temperature:** 400°F

30-MINUTE, DAIRY-FREE, GLUTEN-FREE

If you haven't yet noticed the trend in this recipe book, there are many one-basket meals. As a busy working mother, I find it super important to get home-cooked meals together in less than an hour on busy weekdays. Minimal cleanup is always a plus. This dish is a family favorite.

12 ounces boneless, skinless chicken breast, cubed

1½ pounds Brussels sprouts, halved

1 pound fingerling potatoes, halved

2 tablespoons paprika

1 tablespoon chili powder

½ teaspoon red pepper flakes

¼ teaspoon sea salt

2 tablespoons avocado oil, plus more for misting

1 lemon, cut into wedges, for garnish

1. Preheat the air fryer to 400°F.

2. In a large bowl, stir together the cubed chicken breast, Brussels sprouts, potatoes, paprika, chili powder, red pepper flakes, salt, and avocado oil.

3. Working in batches if necessary, line the air fryer basket with parchment paper. Pour the chicken and vegetable mixture into the basket and cook for 10 minutes. Stir or shake, mist with more avocado oil, and continue to cook for 5 minutes.

4. The meal is ready when the chicken's internal temperature reaches 165°F and the potatoes are fork-tender. Serve garnished with lemon wedges.

VARIATION TIP: You can substitute a different hearty vegetable, such as asparagus or broccoli, in place of the Brussels sprouts and cook for the same length of time.

Per serving: Calories: 378; Total fat: 12g; Saturated fat: 2g; Cholesterol: 72g; Sodium: 275mg; Carbohydrates: 38g; Fiber: 10g; Protein: 35g

Quinoa-Chicken Meatballs with Garlicky Zucchini Spirals

Serves 4 / **Prep time:** 10 minutes / **Cook time:** 20 minutes / **Temperature:** 350°F, then 375°F

30-MINUTE, DAIRY-FREE, GLUTEN-FREE

The air fryer makes cooking meatballs a breeze, and there's no greasy mess or pans to scrub afterward. Cooked quinoa is an excellent binder for meatballs because it provides extra fiber and nutrients. Serving these meatballs over spiralized or ribboned zucchini provides a nourishing low-carbohydrate meal.

⅓ cup dry quinoa

4 medium zucchini, spiralized or peeled into ribbons

2 garlic cloves, minced

2 tablespoons extra-virgin olive oil, plus more for misting

½ cup canned low-sodium chickpeas, drained and rinsed

2 tablespoons tahini

1 tablespoon freshly squeezed lemon juice

¼ teaspoon sea salt

1 pound ground chicken breast

Chopped fresh parsley, for garnish

1. Preheat the air fryer to 350°F. Cook the quinoa according to the package directions.

2. In a large bowl, stir together the zucchini, garlic, and olive oil.

3. Place the zucchini in the air fryer basket and cook for 8 minutes, stirring occasionally.

4. While the zucchini is cooking, in a large bowl, mash the chickpeas with a fork, then stir in the tahini, lemon juice, and salt until well combined and smooth.

5. Add the chicken and cooked quinoa and mix well. Using wet hands, form the mixture into about 16 (1-inch) meatballs.

6. Once the zucchini is done, transfer it to a bowl and mist with olive oil.

7. Working in batches if necessary, arrange the meatballs in a single layer in the air fryer basket. Set the temperature to 375°F and cook for 10 minutes, or until the internal temperature reaches 165°F. Serve the meatballs over the zucchini and garnish with fresh parsley.

Per serving: Calories: 344; Total fat: 16g; Saturated fat: 3g; Cholesterol: 80g; Sodium: 282mg; Carbohydrates: 23g; Fiber: 5g; Protein: 33g

Spaghetti Squash Burrito Boats

Serves 4 / **Prep time:** 10 minutes / **Cook time:** 45 minutes / **Temperature:** 375°F

GLUTEN-FREE

In this mash-up of a burrito bowl and a stuffed squash, the spaghetti squash acts as the serving bowl for ground turkey and black beans with deliciously bold flavors. This recipe gives you everything you love about traditional tacos but with less sodium and carbohydrates. Make sure the spaghetti squash will fit in your air fryer basket. For a large air fryer, a 2-pound squash should fit well; scale down as needed.

1 (2-pound) spaghetti squash, halved and seeded

Extra-virgin olive oil cooking spray

1 pound ground turkey, 99% lean

1 (15-ounce) can low-sodium black beans, drained and rinsed

½ cup chopped red onion

½ cup canned fire-roasted tomatoes

2 teaspoons granulated garlic

2 teaspoons chili powder

2 teaspoons ground cumin

½ teaspoon paprika

¼ teaspoon dried oregano

½ cup fresh chopped cilantro

¼ teaspoon sea salt

1 teaspoon freshly ground black pepper

1 cup low-sodium cheddar cheese

1. Preheat the air fryer to 375°F.

2. Place the spaghetti squash halves in the air fryer basket, cut-side up, mist with the olive oil, and cook for 30 minutes, or until a fork can easily pierce the flesh.

3. While the squash is cooking, in a large bowl, stir together the turkey, black beans, onion, tomatoes, garlic, chili powder, cumin, paprika, oregano, cilantro, salt, and pepper.

4. When the spaghetti squash is done, carefully remove it from the air fryer and use a fork to shred the flesh in the shells.

5. Working in batches if necessary, place the ground turkey mixture in a single layer in the air fryer and cook for 10 minutes, or until the turkey is no longer pink.

6. When the turkey is done, divide the mixture between the squash halves and top with the cheddar cheese. Place the boats back in the air fryer and cook for 5 minutes, or until the cheese is melted. Cut the boats in half crosswise and serve hot.

Per serving: Calories: 475; Total fat: 12g; Saturated fat: 6g; Cholesterol: 79g; Sodium: 380mg; Carbohydrates: 49g; Fiber: 16g; Protein: 45g

Pineapple-Chicken Skewers

Serves 4 / **Prep time:** 15 minutes, plus 1 hour to marinate / **Cook time:** 20 minutes / **Temperature:** 370°F

DAIRY-FREE, GLUTEN-FREE

Using the air fryer for grilling is easy and still gives intense flavor. I suggest marinating this recipe overnight, but if you don't have time, marinate for at least 1 hour for best flavor. Chicken skewers make for a popular dinner, and leftovers can easily be thrown into other dishes or on top of a salad for quick weekday lunches.

16 ounces Brussels
sprouts, halved
lengthwise

3 tablespoons freshly
squeezed lemon juice

1 teaspoon
granulated garlic

½ teaspoon freshly
ground black pepper

¼ teaspoon sea salt

2 tablespoons extra-virgin
olive oil

1 pound boneless, skinless
chicken breast, cut into
1-inch pieces

1 medium red onion, cut
into 1-inch pieces

8 ounces baby bella
mushrooms, stemmed

1 fresh pineapple,
peeled, cored, and cut
into 1-inch chunks
(about 4 cups)

1. In a large saucepan, using a steamer basket, bring water to a boil. Place the Brussels sprouts in the steamer basket, reduce the heat to a simmer, cover, and cook for 4 to 6 minutes, until slightly tender. Remove the Brussels sprouts and set aside to cool.

2. In a large bowl, whisk together the lemon juice, garlic, black pepper, salt, and olive oil, then add the chicken, Brussels sprouts, onion, and mushrooms. Cover and refrigerate for at least 1 hour.

3. If using wooden skewers, soak them in water for at least 30 minutes to prevent them from burning.

4. When ready to cook, preheat the air fryer to 370°F.

5. Thread the marinated chicken, Brussels sprouts, onion, mushrooms, and pineapple onto the skewers.

6. Working in batches if necessary, place the skewers in the air fryer basket and cook for 12 minutes, flipping them halfway through cooking. The skewers are done when the internal temperature of the chicken reaches 165°F.

VARIATION TIP: If fresh pineapple is not available, you can substitute thawed, frozen pineapple or another fresh fruit such as mango.

Per serving: Calories: 410; Total fat: 13g; Saturated fat: 3g; Cholesterol: 96g; Sodium: 267mg; Carbohydrates: 37g; Fiber: 8g; Protein: 42g

Tangy Barbecue Chicken with Broccoli Rabe

Serves 4 / **Prep time:** 5 minutes, plus 2 hours to marinate / **Cook time:** 30 minutes / **Temperature:** 400°F

DAIRY-FREE, GLUTEN-FREE

Barbecue chicken is usually reserved for the warmer months when you can grill outside, but with the air fryer, this easy, healthy, and delicious meal can be made whenever you want. Using skinless chicken legs will cut almost half the fat when compared to chicken legs with skin, and this homemade tangy barbecue sauce cuts down on refined sugar and sodium—truly a guilt-free dish.

1 cup strained tomatoes

⅓ cup balsamic vinegar

1 tablespoon Dijon mustard

2 teaspoons coconut sugar

1 teaspoon ground cinnamon

1 teaspoon paprika

1 teaspoon chili powder

1 teaspoon onion powder

1 pound skinless chicken drumsticks

1 pound broccoli rabe

1 tablespoon olive oil

2 tablespoons pumpkin seeds

1 tablespoon freshly squeezed lemon juice

2 garlic cloves, minced

1. In a small bowl, whisk together the tomatoes, balsamic vinegar, mustard, coconut sugar, cinnamon, paprika, chili powder, and onion powder.

2. In a resealable plastic bag, combine the chicken and barbecue sauce, then transfer to the refrigerator and marinate for 2 hours.

3. Preheat the air fryer to 400°F for 5 minutes. Arrange the drumsticks in a single layer in the air fryer basket and cook for 20 minutes, flipping them halfway through. The chicken is done when the internal temperature reaches 175°F.

4. When the chicken is cooked, transfer it to a dish. In a medium bowl, stir together the broccoli rabe, olive oil, pumpkin seeds, lemon juice, and garlic until well combined. Place in the air fryer basket, set the temperature to 400°F, and cook for 10 minutes. Serve the broccoli alongside the chicken.

Per serving: Calories: 234; Total fat: 8g; Saturated fat: 2g; Cholesterol: 135g; Sodium: 459mg; Carbohydrates: 15g; Fiber: 5g; Protein: 26g

Italian-Inspired Stuffed Peppers

Serves 4 / **Prep time:** 5 minutes / **Cook time:** 25 minutes / **Temperature:** 375°F

30-MINUTE, GLUTEN-FREE

Stuffed peppers are a family favorite in my house. I enjoy mixing up the protein and other fillings in the peppers to create new flavor profiles. I like to use red bell peppers to provide a sweeter flavor, but if you prefer a slightly bitter bite opt for green bell peppers. This recipe includes lots of fresh basil and a lean cut of protein for a healthy meal full of flavor.

½ cup uncooked brown rice

1 pound ground chicken breast

1 cup chopped fresh basil

2 tablespoons dried oregano, divided

¼ teaspoon sea salt

2 cups strained tomatoes, divided

2 large bell peppers, halved, cored, and seeded

1 teaspoon granulated garlic

1 teaspoon red pepper flakes

2 tablespoons Parmesan cheese

1. Preheat the air fryer to 375°F. Cook the brown rice according to the package directions.

2. In a large bowl, stir together the chicken, basil, rice, 1 tablespoon of oregano, the salt, and 1 cup of tomatoes.

3. Divide the chicken mixture between the four pepper halves. Working in batches if necessary, arrange the peppers in a single layer in the air fryer basket, chicken mixture facing up. Cook for 20 minutes, or until the internal temperature of the chicken reaches 165°F.

4. Meanwhile, in a small bowl, stir together the remaining 1 tablespoon of oregano, the remaining 1 cup of tomatoes, the garlic, and the red pepper flakes. When the peppers are cooked through, top evenly with the tomato sauce, sprinkle with the Parmesan cheese, and cook for another 3 minutes.

Per serving: Calories: 294; Total fat: 7g; Saturated fat: 2g; Cholesterol: 83g; Sodium: 287mg; Carbohydrates: 32g; Fiber: 4g; Protein: 31g

Turkey and Mozzarella–Stuffed Zucchini Boats

Serves 4 / **Prep time:** 10 minutes / **Cook time:** 20 minutes / **Temperature:** 375°F

30-MINUTE, GLUTEN-FREE

Skip the starch and use zucchini as a base to hold a delicious filling of peppers, low-fat mozzarella cheese, and ground turkey. This meal is hearty on its own or can be paired with a side salad for an extra serving of vegetables. Cooking is a breeze with the air fryer, and this meal will be done in less than half an hour.

2 large zucchini, halved lengthwise

12 ounces ground turkey, 99% lean

½ cup chopped red onion

1 bell pepper, diced

1 cup crushed tomatoes

2 garlic cloves, minced

2 tablespoons Italian seasoning

1 cup shredded low-fat mozzarella cheese

1. Preheat the air fryer to 375°F.

2. With a spoon, scoop the seeds out from each zucchini to create four "boats."

3. In a large bowl, stir together the ground turkey, onion, bell pepper, crushed tomatoes, garlic, and Italian seasoning. Fill each zucchini boat with one-quarter of the turkey filling.

4. Working in batches if necessary, place each stuffed zucchini boat in the air fryer basket in a single layer and cook for 15 minutes, or until the internal temperature reaches 165°F.

5. When the timer goes off, evenly sprinkle mozzarella cheese over the zucchini boats and cook for another 3 minutes.

VARIATION TIP: Switch up the flavor profile and make a Southwestern-inspired dish by using cumin, paprika, chili powder, and cayenne instead of the Italian seasoning and low-sodium cheddar cheese instead of mozzarella.

Per serving: Calories: 240; Total fat: 7g; Saturated fat: 3g; Cholesterol: 75g; Sodium: 320mg; Carbohydrates: 11g; Fiber: 3g; Protein: 35g

Greek-Inspired Turkey Burgers

Serves 4 / **Prep time:** 5 minutes / **Cook time:** 10 minutes / **Temperature:** 375°F

30-MINUTE, GLUTEN-FREE

I typically make my own burgers from scratch because I like having the option of customizing the burger to my own dietary needs and flavor preferences. Burgers are an easy meal to whip up and cook quickly in the air fryer. These burgers are loaded with feta and spinach and other ingredients typical of Greek cuisine. Serve these burgers over a green salad, in a lettuce wrap, or on a whole wheat bun.

1 pound ground turkey, 93% lean

½ cup low-sodium feta cheese

2 ounces diced kalamata olives

2 cups frozen spinach, thawed

½ cup chopped red onion

1 tablespoon dried oregano

1 teaspoon granulated garlic

½ teaspoon freshly ground black pepper

1. Preheat the air fryer to 375°F.

2. In a large bowl, stir together the turkey, feta cheese, olives, spinach, onion, oregano, garlic, and black pepper. With wet hands, form the mixture into 4 patties.

3. Working in batches if necessary, place the burgers in a single layer in the air fryer basket. Cook for 6 minutes, then flip them over and cook for another 6 minutes, or until the internal temperature reaches 165°F.

AIR-FRYER TIP: Air fryer times may vary, so be sure to check for doneness a couple minutes before the end of the cooking time to ensure the burgers don't overcook.

Per serving: Calories: 280; Total fat: 9g; Saturated fat: 2g; Cholesterol: 90g; Sodium: 557mg; Carbohydrates: 9g; Fiber: 3g; Protein: 43g

Juicy Sun-Dried Tomato Meat Loaf

Serves 4 / **Prep time:** 5 minutes / **Cook time:** 20 minutes / **Temperature:** 375°F

30-MINUTE, DAIRY-FREE, GLUTEN-FREE

Meat loaf is a perfect example of the trifecta of air fryer benefits: It cooks in less than half the time it takes in an oven, stays super juicy, and makes cleanup a cinch. This recipe adds flavor to the meat with fresh veggies and sweet, tangy sun-dried tomatoes. Because I recommend using lean beef for this recipe, choose 100 percent grass-fed beef, if possible, for its higher omega-3 content. Serve this meal with your favorite vegetable side, such as Roasted Root Veggies with Fresh Oregano (page 37).

1 pound 90% lean ground beef

½ cup chopped red onion

1 cup frozen spinach, thawed

1 bell pepper, seeded and diced

1 cup shredded carrots

2 ounces (12 to 15) sun-dried tomatoes, chopped

½ cup almond flour

3 tablespoons dried oregano

2 tablespoons dried parsley

1 tablespoon granulated garlic

1 teaspoon red pepper flakes

¼ teaspoon sea salt

1. Preheat the air fryer to 375°F.

2. In a large bowl, stir together the ground beef, onion, spinach, bell pepper, carrots, sun-dried tomatoes, almond flour, oregano, parsley, garlic, red pepper flakes, and salt until well combined.

3. Divide the mixture in half and shape into two small loaves, about 6 inches by 2 inches. Working in batches if necessary, place the meat loaves in the air fryer basket. Reduce the temperature to 375°F and cook for 20 minutes, or until the internal temperature of the loaves reaches 160°F. Let the loaves rest for 10 minutes before slicing.

VARIATION TIP: For an option even lower in fat, try ground bison in place of beef.

Per serving: Calories: 357; Total fat: 20g; Saturated fat: 5g; Cholesterol: 75g; Sodium: 378mg; Carbohydrates: 15g; Fiber: 5g; Protein: 29g

Garlic and Ginger Bison Meatballs

Serves 4 / **Prep time:** 5 minutes / **Cook time:** 20 minutes / **Temperature:** 400°F, then 320°F

30-MINUTE, DAIRY-FREE, GLUTEN-FREE

Ground bison is an excellent choice for healthy cooking. It's lower in calories, fat, and cholesterol and has higher amounts of protein, iron, and vitamin B$_{12}$ than chicken, beef, or salmon. Bison can be dry if overcooked and not seasoned correctly. This recipe packs in a lot of flavor, and using the air fryer guarantees the meatballs will be the perfect texture. I like to serve them over brown rice for a complete meal.

1 pound ground bison

¼ cup sesame seeds, divided

2 teaspoons coconut aminos, plus 4 teaspoons

2 tablespoons granulated garlic

2 teaspoons freshly grated ginger root

3 scallions, thinly sliced, white and green parts separated

4 cups broccoli florets

12 ounces baby carrots, diced

Extra-virgin olive oil cooking spray

1. Preheat the air fryer to 400°F.

2. In a large bowl, stir together the ground bison, sesame seeds, 2 teaspoons of coconut aminos, the garlic, the ginger, and the white parts of the scallions until well combined. Roll the mixture into 16 (1-inch) meatballs.

3. Working in batches if necessary, place the meatballs in a single layer in the air fryer basket and cook for 10 minutes, until browned and the internal temperature reaches 165°F.

4. While the meatballs are cooking, in a large bowl, stir together the broccoli and carrots, mist with the olive oil, and add the remaining 4 teaspoons of coconut aminos.

5. When the meatballs are done, remove them from the basket and reduce the temperature to 320°F. Working in batches if necessary, place the broccoli and carrots in the basket in a single layer, sprinkle with sesame seeds, and cook for 8 minutes. Serve garnished with the remaining green parts of the scallions.

VARIATION TIP: If you cannot locate ground bison in your local grocery store, you can substitute ground turkey, chicken, or 90% lean ground beef.

Per serving: Calories: 342; Total fat: 16g; Saturated fat: 5g; Cholesterol: 81g; Sodium: 398mg; Carbohydrates: 18g; Fiber: 6g; Protein: 34g

Cheeseburger Salad

Serves 4 / **Prep time:** 5 minutes / **Cook time:** 10 minutes / **Temperature:** 400°F

30-MINUTE, GLUTEN-FREE

This hearty salad will keep you satiated until your next meal. The recipe combines all the flavors of a burger but gives it a healthy twist by mixing it all into a salad. The cheese is optional; the salad still tastes terrific without it. Air frying cuts the fat in the meat by allowing excess fat to drop through to the holding pan underneath.

For the salad

12 ounces ground beef, 90% lean

1 teaspoon freshly ground black pepper

4 cups spinach

4 dill pickle spears, chopped

½ cup red onion, chopped

2 cups cherry tomatoes, halved

¼ cup shredded low-fat cheddar cheese

For the dressing

4 tablespoons reduced-fat Greek yogurt

1 teaspoon Dijon mustard

1 tablespoon low-sodium ketchup

¼ teaspoon granulated garlic

¼ teaspoon paprika

1 teaspoon freshly squeezed lemon juice

1 teaspoon white wine vinegar

1 tablespoon water (optional)

To make the salad

1. Preheat the air fryer to 400°F.

2. Place the beef directly in the air fryer basket and season with the pepper. Cook for 10 minutes, stirring occasionally and crumbling the beef with a wooden spoon.

3. When the timer goes off, remove the beef with a slotted spoon.

To make the dressing

4. While the beef is cooking, in a small bowl, whisk together the Greek yogurt, mustard, ketchup, garlic, paprika, lemon juice, and vinegar until smooth. Add the water, if needed, to thin.

5. To assemble the salad, divide the spinach between four bowls, then top each bowl with the beef, dill pickles, onion, tomatoes, and cheese. Top with dressing to taste.

Per serving: Calories: 234; Total fat: 12g; Saturated fat: 5g; Cholesterol: 65mg; Sodium: 406mg; Carbohydrates: 9g; Fiber: 3g; Protein: 23g

Stuffed Pork Chops

Serves 4 / Prep time: 5 minutes / **Cook time:** 10 minutes / **Temperature:** 375°F

30-MINUTE, GLUTEN-FREE

These Stuffed Pork Chops make an elegant meal, but they are surprisingly simple to create and offer lots of bold flavor. Using the air fryer cuts down on cooking time and makes cleanup a breeze, meaning you can have this special-occasion dish any night of the week. Serve them with Roasted Balsamic-Parmesan Brussels Sprouts (page 35) to complete the experience.

4 boneless pork chops (about 1 pound)

1 tablespoon garlic powder

2 cups frozen spinach, thawed

4 tablespoons ricotta cheese

¼ teaspoon sea salt

4 tablespoons Pesto (page 51) or store-bought

1. Preheat the air fryer to 375°F.

2. Create a pocket in each pork chop by cutting a slice in the middle but not all the way through.

3. Season the inside of the chops with the garlic, then stuff each pork chop with ¼ cup of spinach and 1 tablespoon of ricotta cheese. Secure the open end with a toothpick. Top each pork chop with salt and 1 tablespoon of pesto.

4. Working in batches if necessary, place the pork chops in a single layer in the air fryer basket. Cook for 5 minutes, then flip and cook for another 5 minutes, until the internal temperature reaches 145°F.

VARIATION TIP: For a dairy-free dish, use a plant-based alternative such as Kite Hill nondairy ricotta cheese.

Per serving: Calories: 279; Total fat: 16g; Saturated fat: 4g; Cholesterol: 70g; Sodium: 354mg; Carbohydrates: 7g; Fiber: 3g; Protein: 30g

Chapter 6

Seafood

Lemon-Basil Sea Bass with Roasted Tomatoes

Serves 4 / **Prep time:** 15 minutes / **Cook time:** 10 minutes / **Temperature:** 350°F

30-MINUTE, DAIRY-FREE, GLUTEN-FREE

Sea bass encompasses many different types of fish, including striped bass, black bass, branzino (European bass), and barramundi, any of which can be used in this recipe. Sea bass in general are a lean fish, low in calories and fat. They have a mild flavor and easily take on whatever flavors you add to them. The juices from the tomatoes in this recipe keep the fish moist while cooking. Try serving this with steamed rice.

9 ounces spinach

4 (¼-pound) sea bass fillets

2 tablespoons extra-virgin olive oil

3 tablespoons freshly squeezed lemon juice

2 garlic cloves, minced

½ teaspoon red pepper flakes

½ bunch fresh basil, stemmed and chopped

3 cups cherry tomatoes

1 lemon, cut into 4 wedges

1. Preheat the air fryer to 350°F. Steam the spinach on the stovetop and set aside.

2. Pat the fish fillets dry with a paper towel.

3. In a medium bowl, whisk together the olive oil, lemon juice, garlic, red pepper flakes, and basil. Add the fish and tomatoes to the bowl and allow to marinate for 10 minutes.

4. Working in batches if necessary, line the air fryer basket with parchment paper and arrange the fish fillets in a single layer in the basket. Arrange the tomatoes around the fish and cook for 6 to 12 minutes, until the fish can be flaked with a fork or the internal temperature has reached 145°F. Serve the fish with the tomatoes, spinach, and lemon wedges.

AIR-FRYER TIP: Be sure to have equal-size fillets to ensure even cooking. If the fillets are on the thin side, start to check for doneness after 5 minutes. Be sure not to overcook them, or the fish will be dry.

Per serving: Calories: 247; Total fat: 10g; Saturated fat: 2g; Cholesterol: 60g; Sodium: 157mg; Carbohydrates: 9g; Fiber: 3g; Protein: 30g

Coconut Cod with Amaranth

Serves 4 / **Prep time:** 5 minutes, plus 15 minutes to marinate / **Cook time:** 10 minutes
Temperature: 375°F

30-MINUTE, DAIRY-FREE, GLUTEN-FREE

Cod is a white, firm-fleshed fish that holds up nicely in the air fryer. As an ocean fish, it contains important micronutrients not available from freshwater fish, such as higher levels of iodine, and it is also low in fat. Serve the cod over amaranth, an ancient grain that is naturally gluten-free and has more protein and calcium per gram than milk.

1¼ cups amaranth

1 cup low-fat coconut milk

2 tablespoons extra-virgin olive oil

1 tablespoon coconut aminos

1 dried bay leaf

¼ teaspoon sea salt

4 (3-ounce) cod fillets

¼ cup reduced-fat shredded coconut

1. Preheat the air fryer to 375°F. Cook the amaranth according to the package directions.

2. In a medium bowl, whisk together the coconut milk, olive oil, coconut aminos, bay leaf, and salt. Add the cod fillets and allow to marinate for 15 minutes.

3. Lay the cod on a plate and sprinkle with the coconut, pressing down firmly to adhere it to the fish.

4. Working in batches if necessary, arrange the cod fillets in a single layer in the air fryer basket and cook for 10 minutes, until the top of the fillets turn golden brown and the internal temperature reaches 145°F. Serve the cod over the amaranth.

VARIATION TIP: Amaranth is usually found in the grocery store near other grains like rice; if it's not available, substitute quinoa.

Per serving: Calories: 415; Total fat: 17g; Saturated fat: 7g; Cholesterol: 37g; Sodium: 264mg; Carbohydrates: 43g; Fiber: 6g; Protein: 24g

Cajun Crispy Halibut with Cashew-Cucumber Dip

Serves 4 / **Prep time:** 10 minutes / **Cook time:** 10 minutes / **Temperature:** 370°F

30-MINUTE, DAIRY-FREE, GLUTEN-FREE

Halibut is a white, mild-flavored, meaty fish, which makes it suitable for deep-frying, such as in a fish and chips–type recipe. Halibut is also high in anti-inflammatory omega-3 fatty acids, similar to wild salmon. The air fryer will guarantee the crispy texture you love in fried fish but won't saddle you with the fat calories. Serve with a cooling cashew cucumber dip and Zucchini Chips (page 38).

For the cashew-cucumber sauce

½ cup cashews, soaked in water overnight and drained

2 tablespoons plain nondairy yogurt

3 tablespoons freshly squeezed lemon juice

1 cucumber, peeled and chopped

2 tablespoons chopped fresh chives

For the halibut

1 cup unsweetened almond milk

1 large egg white

¼ cup almond flour

½ cup brown rice flour

1 tablespoon paprika

½ tablespoon granulated garlic

To make the cashew-cucumber sauce

1. In a food processor or high-speed blender, combine the drained cashews, yogurt, lemon juice, cucumber, and chives and blend until creamy and smooth.

To make the halibut

2. Preheat the air fryer to 370°F.

3. In a small bowl, whisk together the almond milk and egg white.

4. In another small bowl, stir together the almond flour, brown rice flour, paprika, garlic, black pepper, oregano, onion powder, cayenne, and salt.

½ tablespoon freshly
  ground black pepper

½ tablespoon
  dried oregano

1 teaspoon onion powder

1 teaspoon
  cayenne pepper

¼ teaspoon sea salt

1 pound halibut fillets, cut
  into 2-inch-wide strips

Extra-virgin olive oil
  cooking spray

5. One at a time, dunk each halibut fillet into the almond milk mixture and then coat in the flour mixture.

6. Mist the air fryer basket with the olive oil. Working in batches if necessary, arrange the halibut fillets in a single layer in the basket, mist the tops with the olive oil, and cook for 9 minutes. The halibut is done when golden brown with an internal temperature of 145°F. Serve the halibut with the sauce on the side.

VARIATION TIP: If you are unable to find halibut, you can use another meaty fish such as cod.

Per serving: Calories: 342; Total fat: 14g; Saturated fat: 2g; Cholesterol: 56g; Sodium: 290mg; Carbohydrates: 28g; Fiber: 4g; Protein: 29g

Sesame Salmon Kebabs with Almond Green Beans

Serves 4 / **Prep time:** 10 minutes, plus 10 minutes to marinate / **Cook time:** 10 minutes
Temperature: 350°F

30-MINUTE, DAIRY-FREE, GLUTEN-FREE

Salmon is high in anti-inflammatory omega-3 fatty acids, so it is a wonderful food to incorporate into a healthy diet. The most common types of wild salmon at the store are king salmon and sockeye salmon, which have different flavor profiles and levels of omega-3 fatty acids. King salmon tends to have a moist and buttery texture, whereas sockeye is an oilier fish and tends to have a richer flavor.

3 tablespoons freshly squeezed lemon juice

3 tablespoons extra-virgin olive oil, divided

3 tablespoons sesame seeds, divided

1 tablespoon granulated garlic

1 teaspoon freshly ground black pepper

1 teaspoon coconut sugar

12 ounces wild salmon, skin removed, cut into 1-inch pieces

2 lemons, cut into wedges

16 ounces fresh green beans

1 garlic clove, minced

2 tablespoons slivered almonds

¼ teaspoon sea salt

1. In a large bowl, whisk together the lemon juice, 1½ tablespoons of olive oil, 1½ tablespoons of sesame seeds, the granulated garlic, black pepper, and coconut sugar. Add the salmon and let marinate for 10 minutes.

2. Preheat the air fryer to 350°F. If using wooden skewers, soak them in water for at least 30 minutes to prevent them from burning.

3. Thread the salmon and lemon wedges onto the skewers.

4. In a separate bowl, stir together the green beans, the remaining 1½ tablespoons of olive oil, remaining 1½ tablespoons of sesame seeds, minced garlic, almonds, and salt.

5. Working in batches if necessary, place the beans on the bottom of the air fryer basket in a single layer and the salmon skewers on top of the beans. Cook for 10 minutes, flipping halfway through cooking. The skewers are done when the internal temperature of the salmon reaches 145°F. Be sure not to overcook them.

Per serving: Calories: 461; Total fat: 23g; Saturated fat: 4g; Cholesterol: 132g; Sodium: 202mg; Carbohydrates: 12g; Fiber: 4g; Protein: 56g

Hummus-Crusted Crispy Shrimp with Mango-Avocado Dip

Serves 4 / **Prep time:** 10 minutes / **Cook time:** 10 minutes / **Temperature:** 400°F

30-MINUTE, DAIRY-FREE

Fried shrimp are delicious but can be too high in sodium and fat for the DASH diet. My recipe uses hummus instead of an egg-based mixture to coat the shrimp and hold the bread crumbs, giving the shrimp a different flavor profile and keeping them moist. The mango-avocado dip provides a delicious sweetness to this recipe without added sugar.

For the shrimp

⅓ cup hummus

3 tablespoons freshly squeezed lemon juice

¾ cup whole wheat panko bread crumbs

2 tablespoons Italian seasoning

12 ounces shrimp, cleaned and deveined

Avocado oil cooking spray

For the mango-avocado dip

2 Hass avocados

1 tablespoon freshly squeezed lime juice

¼ cup chopped red onion

½ bunch cilantro, stemmed and chopped

¼ teaspoon sea salt

1 mango, diced

Freshly ground pepper

To make the shrimp

1. Preheat the air fryer to 400°F.

2. In a small bowl, whisk together the hummus and lemon juice. The hummus will appear thinner than usual.

3. In another small bowl, stir together the panko bread crumbs and Italian seasoning.

4. One at a time, dunk each shrimp into the hummus and then coat in the panko bread crumb mixture.

5. Working in batches if necessary, arrange the shrimp in a single layer in the air fryer basket. Mist with the avocado oil and cook for 8 minutes, until crispy and no longer opaque in the middle.

To make the mango-avocado dip

While the shrimp are cooking, in a medium bowl, mash together the avocados, lime juice, onion, cilantro, and salt. Stir in the mango and season with pepper to taste. Serve the shrimp with the dip on the side.

Per serving: Calories: 349; Total fat: 13g; Saturated fat: 2g; Cholesterol: 161g; Sodium: 354mg; Carbohydrates: 36g; Fiber: 10g; Protein: 27g

Everything Bagel–Crusted Salmon with Kale Chips

Serves 4 / **Prep time:** 10 minutes / **Cook time:** 15 minutes / **Temperature:** 350°F, then 375°F

30-MINUTE, DAIRY-FREE, GLUTEN-FREE

Everything bagel seasoning is a blend of sesame seeds, onion, garlic, poppy seeds, and salt. It's low in sodium and packs a great flavor. I love using it as a crust on many proteins, and using it on salmon is tasty. Kale chips are just that: kale cooked to a crispy, chip-like consistency. Round out this meal with roasted sweet potatoes.

1 pound skinless salmon fillets, cut into 4-inch fillets

2 tablespoons everything bagel seasoning, plus 1 teaspoon

Extra-virgin olive oil cooking spray

1 bunch fresh curly kale (about 6 ounces), stemmed, leaves torn into 2-inch pieces

2 tablespoons extra-virgin olive oil

1. Preheat the air fryer to 350°F.

2. Place the salmon on a plate or flat surface and sprinkle with 2 tablespoons of everything bagel seasoning, firmly pressing the seasoning into the fish.

3. Working in batches if necessary, mist the air fryer basket with the olive oil. Arrange the salmon fillets in a single layer in the air fryer basket, seasoned-side up. Mist with the olive oil cooking spray and cook for 6 to 10 minutes, depending on thickness. The salmon is done when the internal temperature reaches 145°F.

4. While the salmon is cooking, in a medium bowl, massage the kale with the olive oil. Sprinkle with the remaining 1 teaspoon of everything bagel seasoning.

5. Place the kale in the air fryer, set the temperature to 375°F, and cook for 3 minutes, shaking and misting with more oil halfway through the cooking time, until the kale is crispy.

Per serving: Calories: 251; Total fat: 16g; Saturated fat: 2g; Cholesterol: 73g; Sodium: 550mg; Carbohydrates: 2g; Fiber: 2g; Protein: 26g

Salmon with Fig Vinaigrette

Serves 4 / **Prep time:** 15 minutes / **Cook time:** 30 minutes / **Temperature:** 400°F, then 370°F

DAIRY-FREE, GLUTEN-FREE

My huge fig tree left me with a bountiful harvest this year, which meant figs were the star of many of my dishes this summer. Depending on your location, figs may be difficult to locate but are well worth the effort—the balsamic-fig combination provides a sweet and fruity taste that is glorious on fish and vegetables.

For the fig vinaigrette

4 fresh figs

¼ cup balsamic vinegar

3 tablespoons olive oil

For the salmon and vegetables

1 pound salmon, skin on, cut into 4-inch fillets

1 teaspoon paprika

½ teaspoon freshly ground black pepper

16 ounces Brussels sprouts, halved

1 pound sweet potato, chopped into 1-inch cubes

Avocado oil cooking spray

¼ teaspoon sea salt

VARIATION TIP: If fresh figs are out of season, you can use fig jam; just look for varieties with no added sugar. Use about 2 tablespoons and whisk together with the other ingredients.

To make the fig vinaigrette

1. In a high-speed blender or food processer, combine the figs, balsamic vinegar, and olive oil. Blend on high speed.

To make the salmon and vegetables

2. Bring the salmon to room temperature, about 30 minutes. Sprinkle the flesh side with the paprika and pepper.

3. Preheat the air fryer to 400°F.

4. Working in batches if necessary, arrange the Brussels sprouts and sweet potato in a single layer in the air fryer basket, mist with the avocado oil, sprinkle with the salt, then cook for 20 minutes, until crispy and golden brown. Transfer to a large bowl and drizzle with half of the vinaigrette.

5. Line the air fryer basket with parchment paper. Working in batches if necessary, arrange the salmon fillets in a single layer in the basket, skin-side up. Mist with avocado oil, reduce the temperature to 350°F, and cook for 6 to 10 minutes, depending on your fillets' thickness. The salmon is done when the internal temperature reaches 145°F. Serve the salmon over the vegetables, drizzled with balsamic-fig vinaigrette.

Per serving: Calories: 499; Total fat: 124; Saturated fat: 4g; Cholesterol: 69g; Sodium: 296mg; Carbohydrates: 45g; Fiber: 9g; Protein: 29g

Garlic and Herb Fish Cakes
with Yogurt Sauce

Serves 4 / **Prep time:** 30 minutes / **Cook time:** 40 minutes / **Temperature:** 370°F

GLUTEN-FREE

Fish cakes are a great meal to prepare ahead of time for lunches and dinners. You can make a batch and freeze them raw, making an easy meal to heat up quickly in the air fryer. I created this recipe to replace the traditional potato filler with turnip. Turnips are a root vegetable like potatoes, but they have one of the highest calcium contents per gram of any fruit or vegetable.

For the sauce

1 cup plain low-fat Greek yogurt

2 tablespoons fresh dill, minced

1 tablespoon freshly squeezed lime juice

1 tablespoon extra-virgin olive oil

Freshly ground black pepper

For the fish cakes

1 medium turnip, peeled and diced

1 tablespoon extra-virgin olive oil

12 ounces cod

2 large egg whites

1 cup chopped celery

½ cup chopped fresh parsley

To make the sauce

1. In a medium bowl, stir together the Greek yogurt, dill, lime juice, and olive oil. Season with pepper to taste. Let sit for at least 30 minutes at room temperature or in the refrigerator to allow the flavors to combine.

To make the fish cakes

2. In a large saucepan, cover the turnip with water and bring to a boil. Boil for 15 to 20 minutes, until the turnip is soft and easily pierced with a fork. Drain the turnip, transfer it to a large bowl, and mash it with the olive oil.

3. In another large saucepan, bring water to a boil and add the cod. Poach for 6 to 8 minutes, until cooked through. Flake the cod and add to the turnip.

2 tablespoons chopped
fresh chives

½ red onion, chopped

2 garlic gloves, minced

¼ teaspoon sea salt

¼ teaspoon freshly
ground black pepper

1 cup brown rice flour

4. Preheat the air fryer to 370°F.

5. Add the egg whites, celery, parsley, chives, onion, garlic, salt, pepper, and rice flour to the turnip and cod and mix well. Using damp hands, form the fish mixture into about 8 patties.

6. Working in batches if necessary, place the patties in a single layer in the air fryer basket and cook for 10 minutes, until golden brown on top. Serve with the dill-yogurt sauce.

AIR-FRYER TIP: Because the cod is precooked, you do not have to cook the fish cakes for long. Start checking them after 8 minutes of cooking time to ensure the fish does not dry out.

Per serving: Calories: 334; Total fat: 9g; Saturated fat: 1g; Cholesterol: 47g; Sodium: 322mg; Carbohydrates: 37g; Fiber: 3g; Protein: 27g

Crispy Lemon-Dijon Cod with Greek Yogurt Sauce

Serves 4 / **Prep time:** 10 minutes / **Cook time:** 10 minutes / **Temperature:** 375°F

30-MINUTE

Cod is a mild-flavored fish, which makes it versatile in recipes. Cod cooks quickly, so do not overcook it or it will become dry and lose much of its flavor. Plain low-fat Greek yogurt is a healthy food to incorporate into dip and sauce bases because it's high in protein and low in fat and sugar, creating a creamy base that tastes more decadent than it is. This dish pairs well with a side salad.

For the sauce

1 dill pickle, finely diced

1 tablespoon freshly squeezed lemon juice

1 cup plain low-fat Greek yogurt

1 tablespoon minced fresh dill

1 shallot, finely chopped

Freshly ground black pepper

For the cod

3 tablespoons freshly squeezed lemon juice

2 tablespoons Dijon mustard

1 cup whole wheat panko bread crumbs

½ teaspoon garlic powder

½ teaspoon paprika

⅛ teaspoon cayenne pepper

12 ounces cod, cut into 2-inch pieces

Extra-virgin olive oil cooking spray

To make the sauce

1. In a small bowl, whisk together the pickle, lemon juice, Greek yogurt, dill, and shallot until smooth.

2. Season with black pepper to taste and refrigerate for 5 minutes, or until ready to use, to allow the flavors to meld.

To make the cod

3. Preheat the air fryer to 375°F.

4. In a small bowl, whisk together the lemon juice and mustard.

5. In a medium bowl, stir together the panko bread crumbs, garlic powder, paprika, and cayenne.

6. Brush the cod with the lemon-mustard mixture, then coat with the panko bread crumb mixture.

7. Working in batches if necessary, mist the air fryer basket with the olive oil. Arrange the cod in a single layer in the basket, mist the tops with olive oil, and cook for 10 minutes. The cod is done when it is golden brown and the internal temperature is 145°F. Serve with the sauce on the side.

Per serving: Calories: 202; Total fat: 3g; Saturated fat: 1g; Cholesterol: 49mg; Sodium: 524mg; Carbohydrates: 19g; Fiber: 3g; Protein: 25g

Lemon-Herbed Scallops with Mediterranean-Inspired Salsa

Serves 4 / **Prep time:** 15 minutes, plus 10 minutes to marinate / **Cook time:** 10 minutes
Temperature: 350°F

GLUTEN-FREE

Sea scallops are much larger than bay scallops and typically work better in recipes where they are cooked individually. Scallops only take minutes to cook in the air fryer. They are high in magnesium, which is a mineral recommended in the DASH diet due to its contribution to overall heart health. The salsa gives this dish a rustic twist with Mediterranean-inspired herbs such as oregano.

For the salsa

2 ounces reduced-fat feta cheese

2 cups canned low-sodium chickpeas, drained and rinsed

2 large cucumbers, chopped

2 cups cherry tomatoes, chopped

½ cup chopped red onion

1 tablespoon extra-virgin olive oil

½ teaspoon dried oregano

½ teaspoon freshly ground pepper

¼ teaspoon sea salt

To make the salsa

1. In a large bowl, stir together the feta, chickpeas, cucumbers, tomatoes, onion, olive oil, oregano, pepper, and salt and allow to sit for 10 minutes.

To make the scallops

2. Preheat the air fryer to 350°F.

3. Pat the scallops with paper towels to dry any excess water.

4. In a large bowl, whisk together the olive oil, red pepper flakes, lemon juice, and parsley. Add the scallops and allow to marinate for 10 minutes.

For the scallops

1 pound sea scallops

2 tablespoons extra-virgin olive oil

1 teaspoon red pepper flakes

3 tablespoons freshly squeezed lemon juice

¼ cup chopped fresh parsley

Extra-virgin olive oil cooking spray

5. Mist the air fryer basket with the olive oil. Working in batches if necessary, arrange the scallops in a single layer in the basket and cook for 6 minutes, or until the internal temperature is 120°F (carryover cooking will add another 10 to 15°F). Serve the scallops over the salsa.

AIR-FRYER TIP: Allow ½ inch of space between the scallops to ensure they cook properly. Preheat the air fryer so that it sizzles when the scallops are placed in the basket.

VARIATION TIP: To make this recipe dairy-free, substitute ½ cup of kalamata olives, diced, for the feta cheese. If you like a spicy kick, add 1 chopped jalapeño.

Per serving: Calories: 401; Total fat: 16g; Saturated fat: 3g; Cholesterol: 41g; Sodium: 490mg; Carbohydrates: 37g; Fiber: 9g; Protein: 30g

Desserts

DASH Cinnamon Toast Granola

Serves 4 / **Prep time:** 15 minutes / **Cook time:** 10 minutes / **Temperature:** 350°F

30-MINUTE, GLUTEN-FREE, VEGAN

Granola can be a delicious sweet treat. However, store-bought varieties can contain as much sugar as a candy bar. The air fryer is a terrific tool to quickly toast granola, and making the granola at home allows you to control the flavor profile and sugar content, which is a double win. This recipe uses an erythritol-stevia blend (a calorie-free natural sweetener) to sweeten the granola. Make a batch of this granola to have as a high-energy on-the-go snack. Once cooled, it can be stored in an airtight container for 1½ weeks.

2 tablespoons ground flaxseed

6 tablespoons warm water

3 cups gluten-free old-fashioned rolled oats

½ cup chopped pecans

1 cup unsweetened dried figs, chopped

2 tablespoons ground cinnamon

1 tablespoon dried ginger

1 teaspoon pure vanilla extract

¼ teaspoon sea salt

2½ tablespoons erythritol-stevia blend, such as Truvia

¼ cup unsweetened applesauce

1. Preheat the air fryer to 350°F.

2. In a small bowl, stir together the ground flaxseed with the warm water and allow to sit for 10 minutes to thicken.

3. In a large bowl, stir together the oats, pecans, flax egg, figs, cinnamon, ginger, vanilla, and salt.

4. In a separate small bowl, stir together the erythritol-stevia blend and applesauce until the sweetener is dissolved, then add it to the oat mixture.

5. Line the air fryer basket with parchment paper. Working in batches if necessary, pour the granola mixture into the basket and level into an even layer. Cook for 7 minutes, until golden brown.

6. Remove the granola from the air fryer carefully and lay on the counter to cool.

AIR-FRYER TIP: Oats can brown quickly in the air fryer, so be sure not to burn the granola.

VARIATION TIP: For a different flavor profile, substitute walnuts for the pecans and pumpkin pie spice for the cinnamon.

Per serving: Calories: 432; Total fat: 16g; Saturated fat: 2g; Cholesterol: 0g; Sodium: 151mg; Carbohydrates: 75g; Fiber: 13g; Protein: 11g

Blueberry-Chocolate Scones

Makes 4 scones / Prep time: 10 minutes / **Cook time:** 10 minutes / **Temperature:** 320°F

30-MINUTE, GLUTEN-FREE, VEGETARIAN

I am here to tell you: Scones are not just for breakfast. It's a common debate in my household, but I say scones are the perfect vehicle for sweet chocolate chips, making a tasty chocolaty dessert. Applesauce is used in place of the butter typically seen in scone recipes to reduce the saturated fat content. Because these scones are gluten-free, they will be a little more dense than traditional scones but still will have a great flavor.

1 cup almond flour

1 teaspoon low-sodium baking powder

¼ teaspoon baking soda

2 tablespoons ground cinnamon

¼ teaspoon sea salt

¼ cup plain Greek yogurt

¼ cup unsweetened applesauce

1 teaspoon pure vanilla extract

1 cup fresh blueberries

¼ cup dark chocolate chips

Avocado olive oil cooking spray

1. Preheat the air fryer to 320°F.

2. In a small bowl, stir together the almond flour, baking powder, baking soda, cinnamon, and salt.

3. In a large bowl, stir together the yogurt, applesauce, and vanilla.

4. Add the dry ingredients to the wet ingredients and mix well, until a smooth dough forms. Fold in the blueberries and chocolate chips. The dough will be sticky, which is normal.

5. Use damp hands to form the mixture into triangular scones.

6. Mist the air fryer basket with the avocado oil. Working in batches if necessary, arrange the scones in a single layer in the basket, ensuring they are not touching. Cook for 12 minutes, until golden brown.

VARIATION TIP: Change the flavor profile with different berries; mixed berries, blackberries, or raspberries all would work great.

Per serving (1 scone): Calories: 271; Total fat: 18g; Saturated fat: 3g; Cholesterol: 1g; Sodium: 236mg; Carbohydrates: 23g; Fiber: 7g; Protein: 9g

Whole-Grain Banana-Walnut Bread

Serves 4 / **Prep time:** 10 minutes / **Cook time:** 15 minutes / **Temperature:** 320°F

30-MINUTE, DAIRY-FREE, VEGETARIAN

Banana can be used to sweeten recipes instead of sugar. Be sure to choose ripe bananas that have some brown spots to achieve the necessary sweetness, and mash them well before combining with the other ingredients. The air fryer produces a golden outside and moist inside, making for perfect banana bread.

1½ cups whole wheat flour

1 teaspoon low-sodium baking powder

¼ teaspoon sea salt

2 tablespoons ground cinnamon

2 ripe bananas, mashed

3 egg whites

2 tablespoons applesauce

1 teaspoon pure vanilla extract

¼ cup chopped walnuts

¼ cup dark chocolate chips

1. Preheat the air fryer to 320°F.

2. In a large bowl, whisk together the flour, baking powder, salt, and cinnamon.

3. In another large bowl, whisk together the mashed bananas, egg whites, applesauce, and vanilla.

4. Add the dry ingredients to the wet ingredients and mix well until and a smooth dough forms. Fold in the walnuts and chocolate chips.

5. Working in two batches if necessary, arrange the dough in an air fryer baking dish or line the air fryer basket with parchment paper and add the banana bread. Cook for 15 minutes, until golden brown.

VARIATION TIP: To make this gluten-free, substitute 1 cup of almond flour and ½ cup of tapioca flour for the whole wheat flour.

Per serving: Calories: 345; Total fat: 10; Saturated fat: 3g; Cholesterol: 1g; Sodium: 192mg; Carbohydrates: 59g; Fiber: 10g; Protein: 11g

Air-Fried Donut Holes

Makes 12 donut holes / **Prep time:** 10 minutes / **Cook time:** 10 minutes / **Temperature:** 375°F

30-MINUTE, GLUTEN-FREE, VEGETARIAN

Donuts and donut holes are traditional and much-loved sweet treats, but they are not very heart-healthy because they are traditionally fried in oil. The air fryer is a wonderful appliance for making these treats more heart-healthy. This recipe uses low-glycemic ingredients such as pumpkin puree to sweeten the donuts, coconut sugar as the topping, and almond flour as the base. The addition of tapioca flour, a gluten-free starch made from cassava root, helps bind the dough.

2 cups almond flour

½ cup tapioca flour

½ teaspoon baking soda

2 tablespoons ground cinnamon, divided

1 large egg

½ cup pumpkin puree

1 tablespoon extra-virgin olive oil

3 tablespoons Greek yogurt

1 teaspoon pure vanilla extract

¼ cup coconut sugar

Avocado olive oil cooking spray

1. Preheat the air fryer to 375°F.

2. In a large bowl, whisk together the almond flour, tapioca flour, baking soda, and 1 tablespoon of cinnamon.

3. In another large bowl, whisk together the egg, pumpkin puree, olive oil, Greek yogurt, and vanilla.

4. Add the dry ingredients to the wet ingredients and mix well until a smooth dough forms.

5. Using damp hands, roll the dough into 1-inch balls. Working in batches if necessary, mist the air fryer basket with the avocado oil, arrange the donut holes in a single layer in the basket, and cook for 6 to 8 minutes, until golden brown.

6. While the donut holes are cooking, in a small bowl, stir together the coconut sugar and remaining 1 tablespoon of cinnamon.

7. When the donut holes are done, lightly mist them with avocado oil and roll in the cinnamon sugar.

VARIATION TIP: For a different topping, melt dark chocolate and dip the donut holes, allowing the chocolate to harden, instead of rolling in cinnamon coconut sugar.

Per serving (3 donut holes): Calories: 464; Total fat: 30g; Saturated fat: 3g; Cholesterol: 47g; Sodium: 207mg; Carbohydrates: 41g; Fiber: 9g; Protein: 15g

Amaranth and Oatmeal Cookies

Makes 12 cookies / **Prep time:** 10 minutes / **Cook time:** 10 minutes / **Temperature:** 350°F

30-MINUTE, GLUTEN-FREE, VEGAN

Popped amaranth, which is a naturally gluten-free grain rich in calcium, gives these cookies a nutty flavor and toothsome texture. Rolled oats, which are also naturally gluten-free, form the base and increase the fiber content, making this dessert more filling. If you have a gluten allergy, check the product label to make sure the oats are certified gluten-free, as there can be cross-contamination during production.

¼ cup popped amaranth (see end of recipe)

1 cup gluten-free old-fashioned rolled oats

½ teaspoon low-sodium baking powder

1 tablespoon ground cinnamon

¼ teaspoon sea salt

2 ripe large bananas, mashed thoroughly

3 tablespoons unsweetened almond milk

1 teaspoon pure vanilla extract

2 tablespoons almond butter

½ cup dried raisins

Avocado olive oil cooking spray

1. Preheat the air fryer to 350°F.

2. In a large bowl, stir together the popped amaranth, oats, baking powder, cinnamon, and salt.

3. In a small bowl, stir together the bananas, almond milk, vanilla, and almond butter until smooth.

4. Add the dry ingredients to the banana mixture and mix until smooth. Fold in the raisins.

5. Working in batches if necessary, mist the air fryer basket with the avocado oil. Drop dough in rounded tablespoonfuls in a single layer directly into the basket, 1 inch apart, and cook for 8 to 10 minutes, until golden brown.

TO POP AMARANTH: Heat a tall saucepan over medium-high heat. Test that the skillet is hot enough with a drizzle of water, which should bubble right away. Add 1 tablespoon of amaranth to the dry pot. It should start to pop immediately. You may have to throw out the first batch if the heat is not hot enough.

Per serving (3 cookies): Calories: 305; Total fat: 7g; Saturated fat: 1g; Cholesterol: 0g; Sodium: 162mg; Carbohydrates: 58g; Fiber: 9g; Protein: 7g

Caramelized Cinnamon Peaches
with Nutty Vanilla Ricotta

Serves 4 / **Prep time:** 5 minutes / **Cook time:** 10 minutes / **Temperature:** 400°F

30-MINUTE, GLUTEN-FREE, VEGETARIAN

I created this recipe as a simple dessert that can be ready in 15 minutes, a quick solution to an insistent sweet tooth. The air fryer's heat quickly caramelizes fruit to bring out its natural sweetness, no added sugar needed. The cinnamon will also increase the sweet taste without adding sugar.

4 cups frozen peaches, thawed

4 tablespoons ground cinnamon, divided

Avocado olive oil cooking spray

¼ cup part-skim ricotta cheese

¼ teaspoon pure vanilla extract

¾ cup unsalted slivered almonds, for garnish

¼ cup unsalted pumpkin seeds, for garnish

1. Preheat the air fryer to 400°F.

2. Lay the peaches on a flat surface and sprinkle with 2 tablespoons of cinnamon.

3. Working in batches if necessary, mist the air fryer basket with the avocado oil. Arrange the peaches in a single layer in the air fryer basket and cook for 10 minutes, until they start to caramelize.

4. While the peaches are cooking, in a small bowl, stir together the ricotta cheese, vanilla, and remaining 2 tablespoons of cinnamon.

5. When the peaches are done, transfer them to a plate. Scoop a dollop of the ricotta mixture on each serving and garnish with the almonds and pumpkin seeds. These peaches are best served warm, but leftovers can be refrigerated in an airtight container for up to 4 days.

VARIATION TIP: To make this dessert dairy-free, substitute a plant-based ricotta such as Kite Hill's almond milk ricotta alternative. For a nuttier flavor profile, quickly toast the pumpkin seeds and nuts in the air fryer for 4 to 6 minutes.

Per serving: Calories: 260; Total fat: 17g; Saturated fat: 2g; Cholesterol: 5g; Sodium: 28mg; Carbohydrates: 2g; Fiber: 6g; Protein: 10g

Simple Berry Crisp

Serves 4 / **Prep time:** 10 minutes / **Cook time:** 15 minutes / **Temperature:** 350°F

30-MINUTE, GLUTEN-FREE, VEGAN

Wild blueberries are denser in nutrients than regular blueberries because they have less water content. They are typically found in the freezer aisle year-round or fresh during the summer months. They have a sweeter flavor than regular blueberries, which is perfect for this no-added-sugar blueberry crisp! This dessert is quickly cooked in the air fryer and guarantees easy cleanup. You will likely have to split this recipe in half and cook it in two batches.

4 cups wild blueberries, fresh or frozen

1 tablespoon freshly squeezed lemon juice

1 tablespoon arrowroot flour or cornstarch

2 cups old-fashioned rolled oats

½ cup unsweetened applesauce

½ cup slivered almonds

1 teaspoon pure vanilla extract

2 tablespoons ground cinnamon

¼ teaspoon sea salt

1. Preheat the air fryer to 350°F.

2. In an air fryer baking pan, spread out the blueberries, top with the lemon juice, and sprinkle with the arrowroot flour.

3. In a large bowl, stir together the oats, applesauce, almonds, vanilla, cinnamon, and salt until combined.

4. Scatter the topping over the blueberries, ensuring the blueberries are completely covered.

5. Place the pan in the air fryer basket and cook for 15 minutes, until the blueberries are bubbling and the top is golden brown.

VARIATION TIP: To add a tart flavor to this sweet dish, substitute the same quantity of fresh or frozen mixed berries, such as raspberries, blackberries, and/or blueberries, and follow the recipe as written. Or, for a different flavor profile, substitute walnuts for the almonds and use pumpkin pie spice instead of cinnamon.

Per serving: Calories: 325; Total fat: 11g; Saturated fat: 1g; Cholesterol: 0g; Sodium: 152mg; Carbohydrates: 54g; Fiber: 11g; Protein: 9g

Baked Apples with Warm Almond Butter Sauce

Makes 4 apples / **Prep time:** 10 minutes / **Cook time:** 30 minutes/ **Temperature:** 400°F

GLUTEN-FREE, VEGAN

Baked apples are a staple in many households, and using the air fryer can cut the baking time in half. A sweeter variety of apple provides sweetness without adding extra sugar, and subbing out dairy butter for almond butter provides healthy fats in this recipe.

4 Red Delicious or Honeycrisp apples

4 tablespoons natural almond butter

1 teaspoon pure vanilla extract

2 teaspoons ground cinnamon

½ teaspoon ground nutmeg

4 tablespoons walnuts, chopped

1. Preheat the air fryer to 400°F.

2. Core the apples by cutting around the core, down to about three-quarters of the depth. Using a spoon, carefully dig out the core, making sure to remove all the seeds.

3. In a small bowl, stir together the almond butter, vanilla, cinnamon, and nutmeg. Spoon the almond butter mixture into the cored part of the apples.

4. Working in batches if necessary, arrange the apples in a single layer in the air fryer basket and cook for 30 minutes, until the apples are fork tender.

5. Carefully remove the apples and sprinkle the walnuts on top. Serve warm.

VARIATION TIP: If someone in your household has an almond allergy, different nut butters can be used in place of the almond butter. Peanut butter works great as a substitute.

Per serving (1 apple): Calories: 274; Total fat: 14g; Saturated fat: 1g; Cholesterol: 0g; Sodium: 6mg; Carbohydrates: 35g; Fiber: 8g; Protein: 5g

Brownie Bites

Makes 8 bites / **Prep time:** 10 minutes / **Cook time:** 15 minutes / **Temperature:** 320°F

30-MINUTE, DAIRY-FREE, GLUTEN-FREE, VEGETARIAN

Chickpeas are probably not the first thing that comes to mind as an ingredient for baking. However, they are more versatile than just adding them to a salad or making hummus. Chickpeas are a great substitute for flour in baking and provide high amounts of protein and fiber. Give them a try; you likely won't even notice the chickpeas in these delicious brownie bites.

7 pitted Medjool dates

1 cup canned low-sodium chickpeas, drained

2 large egg whites

2 tablespoons olive oil

2 tablespoons unsweetened almond milk

½ cup cacao powder

½ teaspoon low-sodium baking powder

¼ teaspoon sea salt

1. In a high-speed blender or food processor, combine the dates, chickpeas, egg whites, olive oil, almond milk, cacao, baking powder, and salt and blend on high speed until completely smooth.

2. Put about 1 tablespoon of batter into each mini muffin cup.

3. Working in batches if necessary, arrange the mini muffin liners in a single layer in the air fryer basket, set the temperature to 320°F, and cook for 15 minutes, until a toothpick inserted in the middle of the brownie bites comes out clean.

Per serving (1 bite): Calories: 363; Total fat: 12g; Saturated fat: 3g; Cholesterol: 0g; Sodium: 183mg; Carbohydrates: 55g; Fiber: 16g; Protein: 14g

Vegan Pumpkin Muffins

Makes 4 muffins / **Prep time:** 10 minutes, plus 10 minutes to soak / **Cook time:** 10 minutes
Temperature: 350°F

30-MINUTE, GLUTEN-FREE, VEGAN

Pumpkin muffins are not just for the fall! Pumpkin is a great food to incorporate into your diet because it's rich in beta-carotene, an antioxidant beneficial for immunity and eye health. It's also high in potassium, which helps lower blood pressure. This recipe uses a "flax egg," which is a vegan egg substitute perfect for the DASH diet, because it does not contain cholesterol but provides the same consistency and texture as an egg in baked goods.

1 tablespoon ground flaxseed

4 tablespoons warm water, divided

1 cup almond flour

½ teaspoon low-sodium baking powder

1 tablespoon pumpkin pie spice

¼ teaspoon sea salt

1 ripe large banana, thoroughly mashed

½ cup pumpkin puree

3 tablespoons applesauce

½ teaspoon pure vanilla extract

1. Preheat the air fryer to 350°F.

2. In a small bowl, stir together the ground flaxseed and 3 tablespoons of warm water and allow to sit for 10 minutes to thicken.

3. In a large bowl, whisk together the almond flour, baking powder, pumpkin pie spice, and salt.

4. In another large bowl, stir together the banana, pumpkin puree, applesauce, vanilla, flax mixture, and remaining 1 tablespoon of water until smooth.

5. Add the dry ingredients to the pumpkin mixture and mix well until smooth. Note, the dough will be thick and must be spooned into the muffin liners.

6. Fill the muffin liners three-quarters full. Working in batches if necessary, arrange the muffin liners in a single layer (or air fryer muffin tin) in the basket and cook for 10 minutes, until golden brown on top.

Per serving (1 muffin): Calories: 237; Total fat: 16g; Saturated fat: 1g; Cholesterol: 0g; Sodium: 154mg; Carbohydrates: 10g; Fiber: 6g; Protein: 7g

Air Fryer Cooking Chart

The following chart is a general reference guide; your air fryer may require different cooking times and temperatures. Be sure to check the manufacturer's instructions that came with your appliance. It is always recommended to cook meats, poultry, and seafood until they have reached a safe internal temperature. The recipes in this book were tested using a basket-style 6.8-quart air fryer.

FRESH FOOD COOKING CHART

POULTRY	QUANTITY	TIME	TEMPERATURE	NOTES
Chicken breasts (boneless, skinless)	1 or 2 (6-ounce) breasts	15 to 20 minutes	350°F	Spray with oil* and sprinkle with seasonings; flip half-way through cooking time.
Chicken drumsticks, skinless	1 to 4 drumsticks	16 to 20 minutes	400°F	Spray with oil* and sprinkle with seasonings; shake halfway through cooking time.
Chicken thighs (boneless, skinless)	1 or 2 (6-ounce) thighs	10 to 15 minutes	400°F	Spray with oil* and sprinkle with seasonings; flip half-way through cooking time.
Chicken tenders	Up to 4 tenders	8 to 10 minutes	375°F	Spray with oil* and sprinkle with seasonings; shake halfway through cooking time.
Turkey (ground)	8 ounces	5 to 10 minutes	375°F	Spray with oil* and sprinkle with seasonings; shake halfway through cooking time.
Turkey burgers	1 or 2 (4-ounce burgers)	10 to 13 minutes	375°F	Spray with oil*; flip halfway through cooking time.

BEEF	QUANTITY	TIME	TEMPERATURE	NOTES
Ground beef or bison	¼ to ½ pound	8 to 10 minutes	400°F	Stir or shake throughout cooking, until no longer pink.
Meatballs	5 to 10 meatballs	7 to 10 minutes	400°F	Sprinkle with seasonings and flip halfway through cooking time.
Meat loaf	1 (8-ounce) loaf	15 to 20 minutes	375°F	Time will vary depending on the thickness of the meat loaf; use a meat thermometer and cook to internal temperature of 160°F.

PORK	QUANTITY	TIME	TEMPERATURE	NOTES
Pork chops (boneless)	¼ to ½ pound	12 to 15 minutes	375°F	Spray with oil* and sprinkle with seasonings; flip halfway through cooking time.
Pork loin	¼ to ½ pound	50 to 60 minutes	360°F	Spray with oil* and sprinkle with seasonings; flip halfway through cooking time.

FISH AND SEAFOOD	QUANTITY	TIME	TEMPERATURE	NOTES
Fish cakes	1 or 2 cakes	8 to 10 minutes	375°F	Spray with oil* and sprinkle with seasonings.
Fish fillets	¼ to ½ pound	8 to 12 minutes	350°F	Spray with oil* and sprinkle with seasonings; cooking time will depend on the thickness of the fillets.
Scallops	¼ to ½ pound	5 to 7 minutes	350°F	Spray with oil* and sprinkle with seasonings.
Shrimp	¼ to ½ pound	7 to 8 minutes	400°F	Peel and devein; spray with oil* and sprinkle with seasonings.

FRESH VEGETABLES	QUANTITY	TIME	TEMPERATURE	NOTES
Broccoli	1 to 2 cups	5 to 8 minutes	320°F	Spray with oil* and sprinkle with seasonings; cook longer if a crispier texture is desired.
Brussels sprouts	1 cup	15 to 20 minutes	350°F	Slice in half before cooking; spray with oil* and sprinkle with seasonings.
Carrots	½ to 1 cup	7 to 10 minutes	400°F	Slice before cooking; spray with oil* and sprinkle with seasonings.
Cauliflower	1 to 2 cups	9 to 10 minutes	320°F	Cut into florets before cooking; spray with oil* and sprinkle with seasonings.
Eggplant	½ to 2 pounds	8 to 12 minutes	380°F	Spray with oil* and flip halfway through cooking time.
Green beans	½ to 1 pound	5 minutes	350°F	Spray with oil* and shake halfway through cooking time.
Kale	½ bunch	5 minutes	375°F	Trim leaves from the ribs; spray with oil* and sprinkle with seasonings.
Mushrooms	½ to 1 cup	8 to 12 minutes	370°F	Trim stems first; sprinkle with seasonings.
Peppers (bell)	½ to 1 cup	10 to 15 minutes	350°F	Slice before cooking.
Potatoes and sweet potatoes (cubed)	1 to 2 cups	15 to 20 minutes	400°F	Spray with oil* and shake halfway through cooking time.
Potatoes and sweet potatoes (fries)	1 to 2 cups	15 to 25 minutes	380°F	Spray with oil* and shake halfway through cooking time.
Squash	½ pound	12 to 13 minutes	400°F	Spray with oil* and sprinkle with seasonings.

Continued ▶

FRESH VEGETABLES	QUANTITY	TIME	TEMPERATURE	NOTES
Turnips (cubed)	1 to 2 cups	15 to 20 minutes	380°F	Spray with oil* and shake halfway through cooking time.
Zucchini	½ to 1 pound	10 to 12 minutes	370°F	Slice before cooking; spray with oil* and sprinkle with seasonings.

FRESH FRUIT	QUANTITY	TIME	TEMPERATURE	NOTES
Apples	1 to 3 cups	4 to 7 minutes	350°F	Slice before cooking.
Bananas	1 to 3 cups	4 to 7 minutes	350°F	Slice before cooking.
Berries	1 to 3 cups	4 to 7 minutes	350°F	Cook in a baking pan.
Peaches	1 to 3 cups	5 to 6 minutes	350°F	Slice before cooking.

LEGUMES	QUANTITY	TIME	TEMPERATURE	NOTES
Crispy beans, canned	1 to 3 cups	8 to 10 minutes	375°F	Drain and rinse first. Spray with oil* and sprinkle with seasonings; shake halfway through cooking
Baked beans	1 to 3 cups	6 to 9 minutes	375°F	Cook in a baking pan. Spray with oil* and sprinkle with seasonings.
Bean burger	1 or 2 patties	8 to 10 minutes	350°F	Spray with oil*; flip halfway through cooking.

* Use extra-virgin olive oil for low-heat cooking (less than 400°F) and avocado oil for high-heat cooking (400°F or more).

Measurement Conversions

	US STANDARD	US STANDARD (OUNCES)	METRIC (APPROXIMATE)
VOLUME EQUIVALENTS (LIQUID)	2 tablespoons	1 fl. oz.	30 mL
	¼ cup	2 fl. oz.	60 mL
	½ cup	4 fl. oz.	120 mL
	1 cup	8 fl. oz.	240 mL
	1½ cups	12 fl. oz.	355 mL
	2 cups or 1 pint	16 fl. oz.	475 mL
	4 cups or 1 quart	32 fl. oz.	1 L
	1 gallon	128 fl. oz.	4 L
VOLUME EQUIVALENTS (DRY)	⅛ teaspoon	———	0.5 mL
	¼ teaspoon	———	1 mL
	½ teaspoon	———	2 mL
	¾ teaspoon	———	4 mL
	1 teaspoon	———	5 mL
	1 tablespoon	———	15 mL
	¼ cup	———	59 mL
	⅓ cup	———	79 mL
	½ cup	———	118 mL
	⅔ cup	———	156 mL
	¾ cup	———	177 mL
	1 cup	———	235 mL
	2 cups or 1 pint	———	475 mL
	3 cups	———	700 mL
	4 cups or 1 quart	———	1 L
	½ gallon	———	2 L
	1 gallon	———	4 L
WEIGHT EQUIVALENTS	½ ounce	———	15 g
	1 ounce	———	30 g
	2 ounces	———	60 g
	4 ounces	———	115 g
	8 ounces	———	225 g
	12 ounces	———	340 g
	16 ounces or 1 pound	———	455 g

	FAHRENHEIT (F)	CELSIUS (C) (APPROXIMATE)
OVEN TEMPERATURES	250°F	120°C
	300°F	150°C
	325°F	180°C
	375°F	190°C
	400°F	200°C
	425°F	220°C
	450°F	230°C

References

"CDC - How Much Sleep Do I Need?—Sleep and Sleep Disorders." 2019. March 5, 2019. CDC.gov/sleep/about_sleep/how_much_sleep.html.

"DASH Diet and High Blood Pressure." n.d. WebMD. Accessed November 9, 2021. WebMD.com/hypertension-high-blood-pressure/guide/dash-diet.

"DASH Eating Plan | NHLBI, NIH." n.d. Accessed November 7, 2021. NHLBI.NIH .gov/health-topics/dash-eating-plan.

"DASH Ranked Best Diet Overall for Eighth Year in a Row by U.S. News and World Report." 2018. National Institutes of Health (NIH). January 2, 2018. NIH.gov/news-events/news-releases/dash-ranked-best-diet-overall -eighth-year-row-us-news-world-report.

Fischer, Sonja, and Michael Glei. 2015. "Health Aspects of Regular Consumption of Fish and Omega-3-Fatty Acids." *Ernahrungs Umschau* 62(9) (September): 140–51. doi.org/10.4455/eu.2015.026.

Juraschek, Stephen P., Edgar R. Miller, Elizabeth Selvin, Vincent J. Carey, Law-rence J. Appel, Robert H. Christenson, and Frank M. Sacks. 2016. "Effect of Type and Amount of Dietary Carbohydrate on Biomarkers of Glucose Homeostasis and C Reactive Protein in Overweight or Obese Adults: Results from the OmniCarb Trial." *BMJ Open Diabetes Research & Care* 4 (1): e000276. doi.org/10.1136/bmjdrc-2016-000276.

Liang, Hailun, Hind A. Beydoun, Sharmin Hossain, Ana Maldonado, Alan B. Zon-derman, Marie T. Fanelli-Kuczmarski, and May A. Beydoun. 2020. "Dietary Approaches to Stop Hypertension (DASH) Score and Its Association with Sleep Quality in a National Survey of Middle-Aged and Older Men and Women." *Nutrients* 12 (5): E1510. doi.org/10.3390/nu12051510.

Mokhtari, Zeinab, Maryam Sharafkhah, Hossein Poustchi, Sadaf G Sepanlou, Masoud Khoshnia, Abdolsamad Gharavi, Amir Ali Sohrabpour, et al. 2019. "Adherence to the Dietary Approaches to Stop Hypertension (DASH) Diet and Risk of Total and Cause-Specific Mortality: Results from the Golestan Cohort Study." *International Journal of Epidemiology* 48 (6): 1824–38. doi.org/10.1093/ije/dyz079.

Najar-Villarreal, F., E. a. E. Boyle, R. D. Danler, T. G. O'Quinn, T. A. Houser, and J. M. Gonzalez. 2019. "Fatty Acid Composition, Proximate Analysis, and Consumer Sensory Evaluation of United States Retail Grass-Fed Ground Beef." *Meat and Muscle Biology* 3 (1). doi.org/10.22175/mmb2019.06.0018.

Razavi Zade, Mohsen, Mohammad Hosein Telkabadi, Fereshteh Bahmani, Behnaz Salehi, Shima Farshbaf, and Zatollah Asemi. 2016. "The Effects of DASH Diet on Weight Loss and Metabolic Status in Adults with Non-Alcoholic Fatty Liver Disease: A Randomized Clinical Trial." *Liver International* 36 (4): 563–71. doi.org/10.1111/liv.12990.

Rifai, Luay, and Marc A. Silver. 2016. "A Review of the DASH Diet as an Optimal Dietary Plan for Symptomatic Heart Failure." *Progress in Cardiovascular Diseases* 58 (5): 548–54. doi.org/10.1016/j.pcad.2015.11.001.

Soltani, Sepideh, Fatemeh Shirani, Maryam J Chitsazi, and Amin Salehi-Abargouei. 2016. "The Effect of Dietary Approaches to Stop Hypertension (DASH) Diet on Weight and Body Composition in Adults: A Systematic Review and Meta-Analysis of Randomized Controlled Clinical Trials." *Obesity Reviews* 17 (5): 442–54. doi.org/10.1111/obr.12391.

Steinberg, Dori, Gary G. Bennett, and Laura Svetkey. 2017. "The DASH Diet, 20 Years Later." *JAMA* 317 (15): 1529–30. doi.org/10.1001/jama.2017.1628.

Svetkey, Laura P., Frank M. Sacks, Eva Obarzanek, William M. Vollmer, Lawrence J. Appel, Pao-Hwa Lin, Njeri M. Karanja, et al. 1999. "The DASH Diet, Sodium Intake and Blood Pressure Trial (DASH-Sodium): Rationale and Design." *Journal of the American Dietetic Association* 99 (8, Supplement): S96–104. doi.org/10.1016/S0002-8223(99)00423-X.

Watson, Stephanie. n.d. "Do Air Fryers Have Health Benefits?" WebMD. Accessed November 9, 2021. WebMD.com/food-recipes/air-fryers.

Index

Acknowledgments

This book would not be possible without my huge support system.

To my husband, Peter, for always supporting my dreams and being the calming yet reassuring voice I always need. Without your love and support, I wouldn't be where I am today. Thank you for being an amazing father to our daughter and for happily taste testing my experimental recipes, cleaning the endless dishes, and understanding the nonstop grocery deliveries. To Evianna, my daughter and sous-chef, I am so grateful we could spend time together creating and eating all these recipes. You inspire me every day.

To my father-in-law, thank you for your extra time spent with my daughter, so I could get in the additional hours of work and complete this cookbook.

To my mom and dad, for providing me the opportunity to become who I am today and always encouraging my passions along the way. To my sisters, my cousins, aunts and uncles, and friends: I know many of you will purchase this book just to support me, and I truly appreciate that.

Lastly, I would like to thank my editor, Anne Goldberg, for her support and guidance while making the process fun and seamless and Callisto Media for providing me this opportunity.

About the Author

Christina Lombardi, MS, RD, FMNS, is a private practice dietitian and the owner of Functional Nutrition Rx in Babylon, New York, where she provides counseling for cardiometabolic conditions, as well as gastrointestinal health and weight management. Prior to her private practice, she worked as a Clinical Nutritionist for Stony Brook University Hospital's Heart Institute providing medical nutrition therapy for individuals with cardiac conditions such as hypertension, educating them on the DASH diet. She also owns a fitness facility with her husband and is a CrossFit level 1 Trainer at Elevation Fitness and CrossFit.

Visit her at FunctionalNutritionRx.com or follow her on Instagram for more recipes and nutrition tips (@christinalombardird).

CPSIA information can be obtained
at www.ICGtesting.com
Printed in the USA
JSHW011303190422
25076JS00001B/4